Rajesh

AMBASSADOR OF HOPE

Thinking of you,
Be SAFE until we
meet again.
#FAMily

André

AMBASSADOR OF
HOPE

TURNING POVERTY AND PRISON
INTO A PURPOSE-DRIVEN LIFE

ANDRE NORMAN

LIONCREST

PUBLISHING

AMBASSADOR OF HOPE

Turning Poverty and Prison into a Purpose-Driven Life

ISBN   978-1-5445-0723-1   *Hardcover*

978-1-5445-0721-7   *Paperback*

978-1-5445-0722-4   *Ebook*

This book is dedicated to:

Nancy Alper

Dear Brooks,

I pray that as you read this book and learn about my past that you better understand why I want the best for you. My best days in this life began on June 27, and you have been the best gift that God could have ever given me. Know that I love you for you and want you to become the best "you" possible. We all have a past and dark tunnels that we must pass through in this life, but you are the light that gives me hope. Don't try to be me, because you are destined to be greater than me. Always know that I love you.

Dad

CONTENTS

INTRODUCTION

I was being held at MCI-Walpole, a maximum-security prison in Massachusetts, having just been transferred there from federal prison a few months before. I had been in federal custody for two-and-a-half years because, quite simply, the state of Massachusetts couldn't control me. I was too much to deal with. So, they sent me to federal prison in the hopes that I would perish—that I'd be raped, killed, or both.

Instead, I dominated the federal system. I committed too many violent acts to name or count and was kicked out of nine different states. Eventually, the federal system threw their hands up and sent me back to Massachusetts.

Returning there was the equivalent of sending a college kid to middle school. I was so far ahead of everyone—mainly the staff—in terms of what it took for me to run that prison. It was almost unfair. It certainly wasn't fair for the other inmates. The minute I came back, I put my gang together and we took over—the drugs, the extortion, the prison wine, the gambling—all of it. I rolled with my crew. Wherever I went, they went. Whatever I told them to do, they did. Everyone knew it. It was no secret.

Coming back to Massachusetts, I had no property of any kind, so I went on a robbery spree. I beat down ten different prisoners and took everything they had. That landed me a stint in what was called solitary confinement, which was a shock to me. When I had been in Walpole three years prior, nobody cared if a prisoner got beaten or robbed—if someone couldn't hold onto their own belongings, then they didn't deserve to have them. Turns out the game had changed. The then-associate warden pulled me into his office and explained it to me. Because I didn't know the new rules, he let me back into general population with the other prisoners.

Some few days later, I found myself sitting in my cell on a Saturday afternoon, bored and hungry. I decided I would go get something to eat.

I walked out of my cell. I walked down to the gate and I gave the correctional officer (CO) a nod. He opened the gate—I had no pass—and I walked down the hallway to yet another gate. I gave the guard there the same nod as the CO as I walked right past him. Then I walked past two more gates to get to central control, all with no one stopping me.

Central control was essentially a bubble encased in glass and steel. It held computers and camera banks so the guards could monitor everything within the prison walls. From there, they control any and all doors in the prison, especially to places like the kitchen where they didn't want troublemakers—particularly prisoners like me—to get ahold of knives or spices or anything else that can be used to hurt someone.

Another head nod to a guard in central control got me past the gate toward the kitchen. No one was allowed in the kitchen itself who isn't on staff at the prison, and there was a large steel door with a small slot to look through if someone is on the other side. I banged on the door and the CO guarding the kitchen slid the slot open and saw it was me.

He opened the door.

Everyone in the kitchen gave me some form of salute, because the boss—me—was there. I told one of the cooks to make a burger, fries, and a milkshake for me. I stood back and watched while everyone stopped what they were doing to clear space on the grill to make my food.

That's when some guy in a white coat stepped to me.

"Who are you and what are you doing in my kitchen?" he asked me. "You're not even dressed properly. Where is your uniform?"

I looked him square in the face and asked him, "Who the fuck are you?"

He commenced to screaming at me, "I'm the Food Services administrator, and I've got this culinary degree, and I've run that restaurant, and you're in my kitchen, and this isn't right." At that point, not only was I looking at him like he's crazy, but so was everyone else around him. Finally, he says, "I'm going to ask you again—who are you?"

There was a song—"Regulate" by Warren G. and Nate Dogg—that was hot at the time, and for some reason, it popped into my head.

"I'm the regulator," I told him.

"Is that right?" he asked. "And what do you regulate?"

"I regulate whether you go home or not," I said.

When I said it, the color drained out of his face and he asked me what I meant. I told him:

"I could kill you on the spot and that would be that. If I do that, your wife and kids lose a husband and a father. I'm not entertaining your trying to be loud. You ain't tough like that, so let's not be tough. Let's talk like men."

He looked around the room and saw that no one was reacting to what I'd said—that I'd threatened to kill him, and no one said a word. No one did anything.

"After ten years of being locked up for killing you," I continued, "they'll let me back into gen pop. I'll still be in prison, and you'll still be dead. Then I will walk back into this same fucking kitchen, through that same damn door, and I will tell them to make me a hamburger, and that's just how it's going to be. There's really only one question: do I get my hamburger today, or do I get it in ten years? I'm a patient man, so it's your choice."

He stood there, paralyzed. Nothing in his training had ever prepared him for someone like me. He'd never encountered an inmate in full control, which is exactly what I was. The other inmates and staff looked at him like he'd just smacked Mike Tyson and not one of them was going to help stop that ass whipping.

On his hip was his radio with an orange panic button. If he hit it, all the guards would come running and save him. I could see his mind spinning behind his eyes, making calculations. Could they get there before I killed him? Even if they saved him, then what? He'd have to deal with me the next day. While his hand hovered over that radio, I made calculations of my own. Then he made his decision.

He slowly walked over to that grill. He leaned over to the inmate making my burger and said:

"Hey, John. Make him two."

Then he looked back at me and smiled. After that, he walked back into his office and sat down. I can't be sure, but I'm willing to bet his next move was to call his wife, both of them asking themselves what kind of job he'd gotten himself into. Meanwhile, I took my hamburgers, my fries, and my shake back to my cell, and I ate like a king.

Because that's what I was.

ALONE IN A CROWD

But what was I the king of?

I was surrounded by people who would do everything and anything I said. It didn't matter if they were prisoners or officers: my word was executed upon no matter what. I did whatever I wanted without fear of punishment, because even if punishment came, it only meant that I stayed longer in the kingdom I ruled.

Yet that food administrator who I threatened, whose life I held in my hands because of the power I had? At the end of the day, he got to walk out of those prison walls. He got to go through the big fence out front and go home to his family—people that loved and cared about him. Even with my food cooked especially for me, surrounded by people who treated my word as law, I returned to my cell alone, never to know any other life but that one.

It wasn't until I had a life-changing epiphany that I realized that I ruled over nothing. What did all that mean if I had nowhere to go and no one to share it with—there was no one who cared about me or respected me that didn't do it out of fear, or because they had something to gain.

I'll share that story with you, along with many others. Mine is a tale of poverty, violence, and imprisonment that eventually ends in redemption and a life worth living. It is a story of a man who went from having no hope, to becoming an ambassador of it for countless others—from individuals who fought through life just like me, to some of the richest and most powerful people in the world.

This book is intended to offer you medicine for what ails you—to be a source of inspiration for you when you feel crushed under the weight of the world. That's not to say that what you'll read here offers any kind of quick fix. When your doctor prescribes you an antibiotic to be taken for thirty days, do you stop at day twenty? True, you don't feel sick anymore with only ten days left. Why not stop there?

If you're going to fix your situation, you have to be in this for the duration. You can take no shorts if you hope to find resolution. You will see that my journey not only took resiliency, but the willingness to accept help from others. If you are open to accepting *my* help—offered through my story—I will be there with you each step of the way, as long as you make the commitment to stay the course.

If you can do that, then that's what this book will be for you—a promise to be the voice you need to guide you along your path. I'll share with you the often-painful stories of my childhood and adolescence that, while likely very different from the life you might have led up until your current situation, will provide you with insight into your own challenges so that we might make progress towards a solution.

I tell you this as a man who went from poverty and prison to speaking on stage at the London Business School—a corporate audience full of high-end, multimillionaire bankers. I asked them:

"What can I do to make this speech good for you? How can I make this make sense for you?"

"We've been bankers for forty years," they told me. "Don't talk to us in banking terms. Tell us *your* story, and trust that we're smart enough to draw the lines."

That's what I'm doing with this book—I'm going to trust you to draw the lines between my story and yours.

If you're ready to take that first step, then I want to take you back to the early days of my childhood to see how my worldview was shaped, and how it led me on the path to becoming the king of nowhere.

As the saying goes, you can't know where you're going until you know where you've been.

CHAPTER ONE

———

MY LENS

As a young child, there were three rules—three lessons I had learned—that governed my behavior.

It's okay to hit people.

I'll do whatever is necessary to protect myself.

I don't have to explain myself to anybody—I can do whatever I want, whenever I want.

My mother was beaten before my eyes for many years, and so I believed that if a mother can be hit, anybody can be hit. When I rode the bus to and from school, white children would stand on the side of the road and throw rocks at us and call us niggers. When I came home from school one day, when I was in the second grade, I found out my father was gone. No conversation, no explanation that he and my mom were having problems, that I could reach him at his new place, or that he'd come see me so often.

Just gone.

It's okay to hit people, I'm going to protect myself, and I don't have to explain myself. That's the lens I saw the world through as an eight-year-old boy.

My mother married her high school sweetheart, a man who eventually went to prison for robbing banks. Before he went away, she had two children with him. Afterwards, she met my father, a local drug dealer, and had four more children, including me. He was a hustler, whatever that meant.

And he routinely beat her.

Eventually, she tired of the abuse and kicked him out of the house. This was right around the time the busing crisis had begun. So now she's a single mother with six kids, living in the hood. We all know that story, and it's never a good one. By the time I reached the third grade, I couldn't read so I was put in a dummy class, and no one at home gave a shit.

I remember distinctly a time when I was downstairs play-ing some kind of game with my little brother, long before the days of Xbox and PlayStation. My sister came downstairs for my brother and told him they needed him. They wanted one more person for a game they were playing. I told them I wanted to play.

"You can't play," they told me. "This is a word game, and you're dumb."

I insisted that I wasn't, but they took my brother with them and walked upstairs to their room. I ran behind them screaming, "I want to play, I want to play." We all reached my sisters' bedroom door and they brought my younger brother in to sit down. I stood at the door, begging to be allowed to play.

"Spell the word 'how,'" one of them said to me, "and we'll let you play."

I couldn't.

"See?" they said. "You're a dummy." Then they closed the door to their room.

It's one thing to feel invisible—to feel as if you don't exist. There's no denying that that feels terrible. My family *saw* me—and they ignored me. They chose to make me feel as if I didn't matter to them—because I didn't. There are all kinds of abuse, all of them terrible in their own way. To be seen, and to still be ignored, to me, was the ultimate abuse—the worst form of neglect.

My younger brother knew how to read, write, and spell, and I didn't. Yet nobody—and I mean nobody—said, "Hey, we should teach Andre how to read. We should teach him how to count." Nobody thought that if my little brother could do those things by now that maybe I should have been able to as well. No one intervened. No one said a word about it. They were okay letting me grow up like my father—who is illiterate to this very day.

I learned very early on that I didn't count—that I was alone. I was alone in my own little world, because I couldn't do what all the other kids could. I had to live in my head and process everything there because I didn't have the ability to write my thoughts down, or to make any kind of mathematical calculations. Even today, as a grown man, I continue to live in my head because I couldn't break the habit.

I had another brother, so there were three boys and three girls in total. My brothers were both against me. If I had a fight with my little brother and I beat him up, he'd go to my big brother and they'd both come back to beat me down. Sometimes there was no provocation—they'd just do it out of boredom. Both my younger and older brother were physically bigger than me, so I never had a chance at a fair fight. I grew up fighting two people from day one, always against the odds. We would fight. I would lose. They would walk away, laughing. I'd sit in my room, crying, with no one to comfort me. They didn't care. My sisters were older and didn't have time for me. I learned that not only was I alone in a house full of siblings, but that I would suffer alone as well.

That solitude became a theme for my life.

I wasn't the only one to suffer violence in our home, however. My father, for whatever reason, would flare up and beat on my mother. It was the way he communicated when things didn't go his way or when he couldn't make a point with his words. He'd hit her, and he'd hit her, and I'd cry because she was crying.

It happened so frequently, though, that the tears stopped coming. The first time you see it happen, it's traumatic. The second time it happens, you're still in shock, but the shock has lessened. By the fifth time, you say to yourself, "Yo, this shit again?" Your reaction turns to anger. You're no longer crying because you're angry.

Sadly, at that impressionable age, you learn that this is how to communicate. When words don't work, you use your fists. If it's okay to treat a mother this way, well then it must be okay to deal with others in the same fashion.

PROTECT YOURSELF

I didn't understand the busing crisis until I was a grown man.

A federal judge decided that white kids and black kids would go to school together, and he signed a law that affected me. I didn't go to a white school—I went to an all-black school. There was red, black, and green painted on the side of the building.

But my bus went through a poor white neighborhood.

Boston is very small. I lived in a black neighborhood, so if my school bus had gone straight down Washington Street, we would have never seen a white person. For some unknown reason, though, the buses went around Washington, which took us right through the white neighborhood—and that pissed them off.

They realized black kids were coming through their neighborhood and they weren't having it. They lined the streets and stoned our buses as they drove through, screaming "nigger" at us as we passed. They had heard about other white kids doing this on the other side of town and decided they should take up the cause. This was their war. They joined the crusade. No one stopped them. No one stood up and said that isn't right, and so we suffered this, day after day. It was clear then that there would be no Batman, no Hulk coming to save me. The only person that was going to protect Andre was Andre.

Not only was this the case on the bus, but I learned this within the four walls of my own home.

We still lived in a house when I was in the fourth grade. We had oil heat, which was very expensive at the time. Someone left the door open in the middle of a Boston winter. That meant heat—and money—were flying out that open back door.

My mother and stepfather had a sit-down meeting with all six kids to ask who left the door open. Of course, all six kids said, "Not me." Most times, that would have been the end of it. We'd get a lecture and go on our way.

Not that day. That day our folks had decided that someone was going to take the heat—that this had been one occasion like this too many. They weren't going for it. One of us had to admit it. We went in circles, but no one would fess up to it. Finally, my mother and stepfather decided they were going to leave the room and let the six of us work out who was going to take responsibility. They went upstairs and left us sitting at the table.

By now, you can imagine what my brothers and sisters decided.

They told me that I was going to go upstairs and tell our parents that I had left the door open. I told my brothers and sisters that I didn't do it, but they didn't care. They told me that someone had to take the hit for it, and it was going to be me. Either all of us were going to get beatings, or one of us was going to get a beating—so it was on me. No one for all, all for one shit here, even though I was the one for all. I walked up the steps, to my parents' room and told them I left the door open.

Mothers know when you're lying. They can hear it and they can see it. She asked me:

"Are you sure you did it?"

"Yeah, I did it," I said. I knew a beating was coming, and after years of watching my mother get beaten, it was the last thing I wanted. It was the worst thing ever in my mind. The truth was, though, I was more afraid of my siblings downstairs than I was of my parents.

My mother, knowing I hadn't done it, offered me a choice—a beating, or two months in the house on punishment. They thought that there was no way I'd take the two months, with the idea that they'd give me the lightest beating—essentially none at all—because they knew I was saying I did something that I hadn't.

Of course, I didn't know that they knew. How could I? Since I didn't know, I wasn't considering what strategy would work best for me. All I knew was that if I didn't take the grounding, I was consenting to someone hitting me, and I wasn't having that. Before they could blink, I said, "I'll take the two months." I spun around and left the room, leaving them shocked that I'd taken an extended punishment over a thirty-second beating.

Standing up for myself—telling the truth—served no purpose. I had been conditioned by my brothers and sisters to take the path that would keep Andre safe, or at least, as safe as possible. Rather than risk their wrath, I was willing to take whatever punishment my parents would dish out, even if it meant a beating, because a beating from two was far better than a beating from five. When there was an option for no beating at all, I took it.

That's what it took to protect myself in my own home.

"DAD'S GONE"

My father was in my life from the day I was born—until he wasn't.

I was in the second grade, about seven years old, when I came home from school to find out he's gone.

"What are you talking about?" I asked.

"Dad's gone."

I didn't believe it because it didn't make sense. My dad had a tool bench that he kept downstairs, and I ran to it. We weren't allowed to touch his tools. In fact, I remember my brother once getting hit in the head with a screwdriver because he picked up one of Dad's tools. That's how important they were to him.

When I reached the tool bench, I saw that all of his tools were gone. It was then that I understood that he was gone, too. He hadn't spoken to my brothers, or my sisters, or even my mother. He just left.

Imagine going to sleep and waking up the next morning to find one of your feet is missing. Just gone. It was there the night before, but now it's not. It's been there your whole life, and now it's not. How do you make sense of that?

You don't, particularly when you're eight years old. There's a level of shock associated with that kind of realization. In many ways, it was traumatic. I tried to process as best I could at that age, but the truth was, I couldn't. I wasn't emotionally equipped for something like that, so my mind went to all the darkest places.

He doesn't love me.

This is all my fault.

It was never about the problems he and my mother were having, or that maybe there were financial issues, or that mom's husband might be out of jail. I knew, in my young brain, that it had to have been something I had done.

Whatever the reason, the fact of the matter was that he quit—and in doing so, he gave me the license to do the same. His leaving taught me that I can quit on anything at any time for any reason. Not just if things got too hard. I didn't need any justification.

The reason my dad hit my mom had nothing to do with me. The reason kids threw rocks at our bus had nothing to do with me. The reason my father walked out and never said a word had nothing to do with me.

My father was horrible with emotions and was a bad communicator—that's why he hit my mom. A federal judge decided that white kids and black kids would go to school together, and so white people's way of life was challenged. They protested by throwing rocks at our bus, even though our bus wasn't taking us to their school.

Somehow, I always seemed to end up in the way of other people's shit.

Of course, at that age, I didn't see that it wasn't my fault. The problem with that was my frame, my worldview—my lens—was so fundamentally shaped by these experiences. In many ways, it's fair to say my outlook was severely misshaped by these experiences, because nothing about them gave me the right way to view the world.

In South Boston, there is an actual beach called D Street Beach. It had been there all throughout my childhood, yet I hadn't seen it until I was thirty-two years old. As a black child in Boston, we didn't have the beach.

We had Houghton's Pond.

Houghton's Pond was thirty miles south of the city. It was dirty. There was horseshit in the water. Rainwater. Yet there were people swimming in a beach, not far from the airport—someplace I never had reason to go as a kid—that I never knew was there.

I was shocked the first time I saw D Street Beach. I thought it had somehow been built with all of the other expansions they made in the city and I just never heard about it. Remember that I came up in a time where I couldn't walk into a hotel and reserve a conference room. I couldn't go to a restaurant and have all white people serve me my food, and at the time of writing this, I'm only fifty-one years old.

The truth is that I grew up in a bubble of chaos and poverty and that bubble shaped me until it could no longer hold me.

CHAPTER TWO

———

I QUIT

In elementary school, everyone is little. Even the big kids are little, because they are young-minded. The oldest kids, the fifth-graders, in elementary school were about ten years old. With no internet back then, all we knew as entertainment was the playground. We'd go to school, go home, and then come back to the playground.

When you get to middle school, the oldest kid is now fourteen years old—unless, of course, you got some repeaters, in which case you got some kids as old as sixteen. Anything they do, anything that's important to them, trickles down to the sixth graders. Fashion. Culture. Attitude. Clothes. Pecking order. All those things matter now. As long as you could kick a ball in the fifth grade, life was good. Not in the sixth grade. You had to be cool, fashionable, and hip.

You can guess why I had problems.

When I got to middle school, I didn't know that we didn't have cool clothes, because nobody in elementary school cared. I got old clothes. I got old shoes. There was no one in my house who taught me good hygiene. I went to school not knowing what deodorant was. Didn't brush my teeth enough. Hair was crazy. Clothes were dirty. I played in the dirt all day and then got up to go to school. In elementary school, no one said a word about it.

In my house, people didn't wash clothes. We had a hamper in the bathroom. You wore your clothes and you threw them in there. Wear your clothes, throw them in the hamper. Repeat. Keep that up, and at some point, you run out of clothes. So, what do you do? You go back to the hamper to find something to wear. The dirty, sweaty socks. Towels. Everything is collecting together in that hamper. That meant my options were to wear them again, or no clothes at all—which meant I went to school filthy and smelling terrible.

By the time I got to middle school, they started making fun of me.

"That kid is dirty."

"Look at his pants."

Of course, in my mind, I'm wondering what the big deal is. *I was playing yesterday. What were you doing?* I didn't know I was supposed to come to school with clean clothes every day. I thought you played and kept going. Not even the teachers in elementary school told me any differently.

When I got to middle school, the kids were vicious. They started giving me the business for being dirty. For being poor. For not having. Before this, I never wanted anything. Now, I came home to my mom with, "I need all of this stuff to be cool—these pants, these shirts, these jackets, this hat, these socks, this bag." The list was endless.

She looked at me like I was crazy.

"I got to feed you," she said. "You all break shit all the time. You all cost a lot. I can't afford that, so you got a choice. You can have food and lights, or you can have all that stuff."

I said, "I'll take the stuff."

She said, "Get out my face."

"WHO NEEDS A FREE LUNCH FORM?"

I didn't know what a free lunch was. In elementary school, lunchtime came, and they gave you food.

In middle school, you had to fill out the form. You had to physically take it home, have your mother sign it, and bring it back. Maybe they filled it out for you in elementary school—I never really knew. Either way, it was announced, in front of everyone, that I was one of the kids who needed to take home the form.

It was the most embarrassing thing I'd ever experienced up to that point in my life. I had to get up and walk to the front of the room, take this welfare form, and sit back down, everyone's eyes on me. I'm already seen as the dirty and dusty kid. I'm already uncool. Now I had this indignity to add to the list.

Every day that I didn't return the paper, the teacher gave me the business.

"Where's your form, Andre?" she'd say. "Where's the form? You have three more days before you have to pay for your lunch, and you *can't* pay for your lunch, so you better bring that form back to me."

I hated her.

Finally, I got the form signed. After that, I went down to the cafeteria at lunchtime, where they had these huge books—way before the days of laptops and iPads—where they kept a list of every student who was on the free lunch program. Each day, I had to approach the woman who managed the book and stand there while she flipped through to find my name and check it off. It was humiliating.

To make matters worse, the cafeteria team—or the "lunch mothers" as we used to call them—would make Italian sheet cakes. They'd put delicious looking icing on them and cut them up to sell them for twenty-five cents apiece. I would come through that line every day, just staring at that cake. Chocolate one day. Yellow cake another day. Vanilla the next. I'll never forget the first time I picked up a piece of that cake when I got to the end of the line.

"That's a quarter," they told me.

I told them I didn't have it.

"Then put it back," they said.

I used to do everything I could to try to get a quarter so I could buy a piece of that damn cake. It never happened though. All the while I'm seeing these kids who can have the cake—and all the other things they have. The designer clothes. The new shoes. The watches and other jewelry. Book bags and pencils.

They're clean.

Then I looked at myself and I saw I didn't have any of that—and it started to add up. I became invisible. It wasn't just that they made fun of me, which they did. It was that it became crystal clear how different I was—how I would never have what they had. Nothing good was happening for me emotionally in school.

I didn't want to go anymore.

AN OFFER

One of the few friends I had at the time told me that someone in his family had a hookup. We could get plugged-in to become drug runners in the park.

Back in the day, there were rules on the street. The younger kids could hustle until 6:00 p.m. After that time, all the little guys had to get off the block and that's when the older kids came out. Whatever older meant, I don't exactly know. I just knew we were the little kids and we had to go home.

At any rate, my friend's family member had it hooked up. After school, we could go to the park and be runners. Whoever the drug buyers were, they would pull up and tell me, "I need five bags of weed." I'd run and get the five bags, or two bags, or whatever else they needed, and at the end of the day I got paid.

All of a sudden, I've got enough money to buy the clothes I want. I have enough money to buy all of the things I need. I can go through the lunch line, pay for my own food, and—you guessed it—buy as much of that damn sheet cake as I wanted. It was all good—except it wasn't. I was in a place where I was accepted, but it was for all the wrong reasons.

I didn't have to end up there. In fact, there were people along the way who *did* try to help me. While I didn't have any real athletic abilities at the time, I did well academically, and a few of my teachers saw a great deal of potential in me.

One in particular was Ms. Oliver.

While I was in the dummy class, the teacher there took a vacation, so we were placed in another classroom with a teacher—Ms. Oliver. I had no discipline, so I was jumping around the room, acting stupid. She told me to sit down. I said, "You know I'm from the dummy class, so what do you want from me?"

She grabbed me and slammed me into my chair. "I told you, sit down," she said. "You're not acting the fool on my watch."

Immediately, I thought: am I going to get beat like my mom used to? Is this my turn?

I was terrified.

But then, she did me the biggest favor anyone has ever done for me—she took me out of the dummy class and put me in hers.

"You're not a dummy," she said. "You just learn differently."

She took the time to teach me my learning style. At first, I did whatever she said out of fear, because I was scared I was going to get hit. Then, I did whatever she said out of respect, because she kept showing up for me. By the end of the school year, I ran to her class because I knew she loved me. She had taught me how to read and write. When the year was finished, she said something I'll never forget:

"This is your style. This is who you are. Don't let anybody take it from you."

She wanted to see me succeed. The problem was that I always looked for a way to opt out.

In Mr. Herman's seventh grade class, I hit another kid in the head with a book. Instead of chalking it up to my being a bad kid, Mr. Herman recognized that I had it rough. He was the track coach and decided to put me on the team. After some training, I ran my first race and did well. However, the second time I ran, it was a long-distance—something I hadn't trained for—and I got blown out. I got so embarrassed that I ran straight out of the stadium and never returned to track.

Mr. Herman tried to talk to me afterward—in much the same way all of the other teachers did. They spoke to my gifts, saying that I was gifted, that I was athletic, intelligent, and articulate—that I could be doing so much better, so much more than I was doing. What they weren't doing was helping me process my pain.

I didn't want them to save me—I wanted it to be my father who did that.

I was alone. I had no support, no guidance. The people who were trying their best to provide it for me couldn't speak to that which was hurting me the most. To their credit, I don't think I could have told them, because I don't know that I knew it myself. I wanted my father to be my savior, not them.

Ironically, though he no longer lived with us, we still saw my father from time to time. He showed up at the house sporadically. We got to go visit him every now and then, though he did nothing when we were there. He'd sit in his room the entire weekend. Yet he was still Dad. I knew no other—he was it. All I wanted him to do was wake up one day and say:

"You know something, son? We got this."

I never wanted that spot to be filled by someone else. I waited and waited for him to be the one. I just knew that, eventually, he was going to show up. He might have told me once that he was coming for me, in my child's mind, I latched onto that and kept it in my subconscious that it would someday be true.

Of all the things I remember that my stepfather did for me, it was that he taught me to tie my shoes. He actually took the time, and it meant so much to me. I don't remember shit else that he taught me, but I remember that. He had had enough of me trying and failing to tie them myself, and he decided to teach me himself.

As much as it meant to me, I wanted that moment to be with my father. It sounds so simple, but to me it was huge. Still is. I wanted a lifetime of those memorable moments with Dad. Instead, the moments that I remember are all about the times he failed me.

As a result, I pushed everyone away. I wouldn't do anything anyone thought I was capable of—wouldn't participate in anything—because it wasn't with him. Even as a man now, I'm doubling down on wanting him to have been there. I didn't make the connection at the time—that

I was waiting for him. Until I made that connection, I couldn't change my direction.

LEADING BY EXAMPLE

Due to the standard he'd set for me, I quit—on everything. Because he up and left one day, I could do the same. I didn't stay in the band. I didn't stay in the drama club. I didn't try out for sports.

I didn't do anything.

My father once took me when I was a little kid to a football field. There were a bunch of kids playing there, so, of course, I thought I was going to get to play football. I thought, *Oh my God. Dad is so cool. He brought me to a football game.* My head started spinning with thoughts of all the things I was about to do—and then we left. He'd only brought us there to pick something up for himself.

I continued wishing for him to take me to these places—to do these things. So, in the interim, I quit everything.

Because my father showed me I could.

TIME

Children don't want what parents think they want. They'll

say they want the newest toy, or they'll ask for the latest fashion design—the hot new sneakers, the coolest new style of jacket, whatever. In reality, there's one thing they want from their parents more than any of that.

They want their parents to spend time with them. They want them to spend that time with them to give them their approval—to see that they're not a disappointment to them. When they're down, be it they're hurt, or they're scared, sad or upset, they want their parents to swoop in and save them.

The kids I saw when I was coming up, that were running drugs with me? The older ones that were getting high? That was all a by-product of the emotional unrest in their lives. In selling, running, or taking drugs, they were quitting. They, like me, had no one there—the most important person, the one who was *supposed* to be there—to save them.

They continued on that path because they were in pain. The drugs, the crime—none of those things had anything to do with being cool. In essence, it became a matter of, "If you're not going to pay attention to me, if you're not going to hold my hand, if you're not going to even have a conversation with me and tell me why you left?

"Then I'll show you. I'll teach you a lesson you'll never forget."

Parents are the model for their children. They are the center of their kids' universe. They revel in the fact that they look like their parents. They look to their behavior to model their characteristics—their personality traits and quirks. It's fun to them, a source of pride to be able to be like the people they admire so much. As they get older, they measure themselves against you. *Are my shoes bigger than Dad's now? Am I taller?*

When parents remove themselves from the equation, who will the child measure themselves against?

The things they need to learn most in life from their parents? They're going to learn them someplace else because their parents didn't teach them. The power is given to other voices saying, "Try this drug, take this drink, have sex." When children are young, they ask what seems like thousands of questions per day of their parents. When they get older, those questions slow down—maybe even stop.

That doesn't mean they don't have questions anymore. It means they're getting answers somewhere else. They stopped asking their parents because their parents' answers started changing or—worse yet—they never come.

HE NEVER CAME BACK

There were three graduations that were important when I was a kid—fifth grade, eighth grade, and twelfth grade.

Because there were six of us, there were always two graduations per year. Someone was always graduating from elementary and middle school. I have three sisters, and we only skipped a year in terms of when it was someone's turn to move up.

When it was time for my fifth-grade graduation, no one came.

I was devastated. Even in the span of all the things that have happened to me in my life, I still remember it as one of the worst days of my life. I sat in that auditorium and nobody was there to clap for me, to encourage or celebrate me. It was a solid reinforcement to the idea that I was alone and that I mattered to no one.

Things were different for my eighth-grade graduation—or so I thought.

My father showed up to our house and picked me up for the ceremony. I remember distinctly that he was in a white truck—it stood out because I knew he didn't own a white truck. We drove together to the graduation site,

Faneuil Hall in Boston. All along the way, he's talking to me, telling me how glad he is that I'm graduating.

That he was proud.

Then he tells me he hired a photographer to take pictures during the ceremony. I couldn't believe it. Finally, he was doing all of the things I wanted him to do. He showed up. He was proud. He was even paying for someone to take pictures to remember the event. I couldn't get over how happy I felt, and how great I thought my father was in that moment.

We pulled up to the hall. I had on gray pants, a blue jacket, and blue dress shoes. As I opened my door, he says "I'm going to let you out here so I can go and park. I'll see you inside."

"Cool," I told him.

I went inside and they lined us up for the ceremony. It was a beautiful venue. Faneuil Hall is a historic spot in Boston. I don't know how the school arranged to have the graduation at that location, but there we were. My mother was there. Some of my sisters and brothers actually came, too. Even though they managed to make it to this event, I didn't care. I was looking for Dad. I was waiting for Dad. Dad was coming to see me.

I looked all around. I saw men up in the upper levels taking pictures, so I tried to figure out which one was the photographer my father hired. Still, I kept looking for Dad—and I never found him.

That's when I realized he wasn't coming in.

He wasn't even dressed to come in. He had on work clothes, driving a work truck. I knew then that none of those photographers had come for me. I don't know why he even bothered to give me a ride to graduation. It was in that moment that any expectations I had for my father dissipated. I knew then that he would never be there for me.

Even after that day, he'd randomly stop by the house. He'd stand in the doorway and tell me that he'd be back on Saturday to come and get me, so we could spend time together. I'd simply say:

"Dad, it's alright. Stop with the promises. You don't have to come"

He wouldn't hear that. "No, no, I'll be here," he'd say. "If I don't make it, it's because my truck blew up."

To this day, my mother and I have a running joke, starting back in the eighth grade, about the condition of his truck, depending on where he said he would be. What's worse, the next time he did show up, he'd act as if the time before never happened. Never an apology. Never an "I didn't mean it." Nothing.

I gave up on him then. I decided from that point on that I would reject him before he ever had the chance to reject me. I don't know if the relationship had been severed in his mind or not, but it was for me.

Later, in the tenth grade, something happened at school—I can't recall what—where the office said they were going to call my father. I told them not to—that he wasn't my legal guardian and that he meant nothing to me. They called him anyway and told him I said that. When he came, he asked me if I'd actually said that.

He was bigger than me, and I was afraid of him, but I told him that I'd said it and I'd meant it.

FIRST YOU STUMBLE

So, there I was. I had given up on my father, which meant I had given up on myself. Once that happened, it became easier and easier for me to follow the wrong path. First, I learned it's okay to hit people—it's a natural progression from there to feel that it's okay to shoot people. To dominate anyone around you without ever having to explain yourself. To simply run over anyone in your way.

It didn't happen overnight, though. The damage that had been done, when that last straw hit my back that graduation night, was a pebble in a pond that sent ripples outward—ones that would continue on and carry me into a dark and terrible future.

It started that very next year, in the ninth grade.

CHAPTER THREE

———

THE FALL

Just before eighth-grade graduation, I had to fill out a form to go to the next school. Elementary to middle school happened automatically, but to go to the high school, there was paperwork involved. This form gave me three options: I could go to my district school, and then I could choose two other possibilities. If you didn't fill out the form, you were automatically sent to your district high school.

I didn't care about the form.

My whole neighborhood went to West Roxbury High School. All of my sisters went there. My brother. My neighbors. Everyone. So, I was going to go there. It was just what everyone did. Just before graduation, however, Mrs. Ellis, my music teacher at the middle school, pulled me aside and told me that I couldn't go there.

"Why?" I asked her.

"I want to send you to another school," she told me.

I didn't understand what she meant. "You are a musician," she said. "You have the gift." She had determined that I had a talent for the trumpet. In fact, she felt I was excellent with the instrument. She wanted nothing more than for me to go to a school where I could let my talent flourish and truly take hold. Her husband was the music teacher at the high school she had in mind, and she wanted me to be in his class and his band. She made me fill out the form and select Madison Park magnet school. To my surprise, when I submitted it, I got accepted. I went there and joined her husband's band.

When I got there, I was surrounded by nerds—kids that were nothing like me or the kids that I ran with. Still, they let me stay because the band teacher was Mrs. Eilis's husband, and because I really *was* that good at the trumpet. In the morning, I hung out with the nerds.

Come the afternoon, I was hanging with the tough guys again. At this point, I'm not just running drugs—I'm selling them. I'm carrying guns. I couldn't let go of it just because I'd joined the band. It had become a part of who I was—the identity I'd adopted by giving up. I lived in two worlds—one world with the nerds, one world with the tough guys.

Hanging with nerds was cool to me, too, because it was easy. It wasn't work. I was the coolest guy there and I was great at my instrument. Life with the tough guys was fun. We'd sneak out of school. Hangout in stores and steal things. Just doing dumb shit.

One day, those worlds intersected.

WHAT'S IN THE BOX?

It wasn't long before one of my boys noticed the case for my trumpet.

"What's that box you carrying, Dre?" they'd ask me.

I'd act like I didn't know any better. "What are you talking about?"

"Every time we see you, you carrying that big-ass box."

"Oh," I said. "That's my trumpet."

They laughed.

"Man, that's stupid. Black people don't play the trumpet. You can't do nothing with that."

I didn't know how to defend that. Back then, I didn't know

any black musicians. I didn't know about Miles Davis, the Marsalis brothers, or Dizzy Gillespie. We didn't have the exposure to information online like we do today. I just saw pictures of the guy with the big cheeks. I wasn't an avid reader, so I didn't know shit about him. All I knew was that I played the trumpet because Mrs. Ellis made me play it in middle school. I just played. I was a natural. I was on punishment all throughout middle school, so I played the trumpet. I didn't read music, so I learned to play by ear. Back then I loved *Rocky* and the music from *Star Wars*, so I learned it by playing seven days a week.

My boys gave me an ultimatum. I had to get rid of the trumpet or get rid of them. It was that simple.

Here I was, a kid in ninth grade at a school where I didn't know anybody, except for the people in the band. These tough guys were my new friends. I had figured out in the third grade that I was alone—that I was on my own and had no one I could depend on. I couldn't bear the thought of not having friends, of being alone again, especially at that age.

I gave up my trumpet.

4:00 P.M.

Growing up poor is horrible. People have done it and

made it. Growing up without a dad sucks. People have also done it and made it. Growing up in the inner city can be terrible. It's hard, but people have done it and made it.

You can't make it without a dream. It's just not going to happen. When I gave up that trumpet that day, I gave up my dream—or the hopes of ever having one. I gave up on my only chance at having something that was going to give me some form of guidance and direction.

The trumpet had me on a course to something, even if I didn't know it or understand it. When I gave it up, that one little light I had was gone. I had no place I had to be at a certain time or a certain location. I had no purpose. I was aimless.

I drifted.

It wasn't long before I ended up with my first arrest, that very same freshman year. I beat the hell out of the senior class president. That was the first case I ever caught. They wanted to kick me out of the school system then and there. To this day, I don't know why they didn't. Maybe they, like some others, had seen that hidden potential in me. Whatever the case, I was determined to keep it hidden.

That case got me 350 hours of community service, washing police cars, mopping up the cells at the police station, and cleaning at the courthouse. We had to report there every day to wash the cars in the lot, including those that belonged to the judges and DAs. Then we would go next door to the police station and do my work there.

At 4:00 p.m. each day, a van would show up. They would park on the side of the courthouse, and the guards would go inside to get the prisoners. They'd come out with shackles and waist chains on, linked up to each other.

It was the most amazing thing I'd ever seen.

Every day at 4:00 p.m., I made sure I was out in front of the courthouse so I could see these guys walk out to the van. I couldn't not see it. I'd never seen anything like it. It was like a car crash, where you don't want to look, you know you're not supposed to, but you keep doing it anyway. I'd sit under the same tree each day, waiting and watching. If I missed it, I'd be angry with myself. It was like going to the movies every day.

It wasn't the first time that kind of fascination surfaced for me.

Back in the day, every neighborhood had *the guy*. You go someplace and people knew him by name, and that name carried a reputation. He was the guy that represented that section of town. Our guy was a kid named Dominic Williams.

He was five years older than us, and to see Dominic in the neighborhood was a big thing. We'd catch a glimpse of him riding on his dirt bike or driving in a stolen car. We'd all be excited and proud, telling everyone we'd seen Dominic that day.

Dominic didn't know us from Adam. Never spoke to us, never had a conversation with us. Still, he was our default big brother. We knew who he was, and that when his name was spoken, it meant something.

He was eventually arrested for murder and sent to prison. At twelve years old, my boys and I would sit around and talk about what Dominic might be doing that day—what life was like for him locked up. Already, at that young age, we're already talking about prison. It's a part of my vocabulary. It's in my subconscious mind—a planted seed.

Dominic made it glamorous. We looked up to him, so it only made sense that we would look at prison as some kind of accomplishment. Not even teenagers, we're hanging around a mailbox, talking about a man in maximum-security prison for killing another human being like he's someone to look up to.

With no father in the picture, I had no one to tell me differently.

Quitting creates a law of attraction. Everything around you is going to quit—going to fold in and fold up. If you're not trying, nothing around is going to work. If you're not believing, no opportunities will open up around you. Your world starts caving in. When my father finally made me "tap out" on life, everything went black. I faded away like a ghost for the next four years of high school.

I hurt almost everyone I came in contact with. The lesson I learned from my father about it being all right to hit people had turned into something more sinister. I would no longer hit only to protect myself. I would dominate everyone in my path. My whole attitude scaled-up to a point where it was out of control.

The problem there is that "out of control" has a fan base. It has a space. Go to the bar and drink three kegs worth of beer. People will cheer for you and wait and hope for you to come back tomorrow. When you do, not only will they cheer you on again, but they'll buy you drinks. You're doing the most destructive thing possible for yourself and they want to see you do more. You keep sinking and finding new ways to fuck up, new ways to get yourself in trouble, and new ways not to succeed—and the crowd will urge you to keep going in that direction.

Winners find a way, while losers find excuses. Losers will find every reason and excuse not to succeed. It's only by accident that losers get older. They don't grow. They just age, as a matter of natural progression.

My father was supposed to be my light post. When he gave up on me—when he quit—my world crumbled, piece by piece. Whether he didn't know, or he just didn't care, his presence mattered. When he took it away, it created an atmosphere of chaos, and taught me that the only person I had to look out for was me. Instead of working with my siblings to make life better for us, we did nothing but fight.

My brother and I would come home from school to find there would be no food. It was a toss-up as to who—if anyone—would eat that day. I'd go to the kitchen and, if I was lucky, I'd find some cereal and grab it. Then I'd go to the refrigerator only to see that there was no milk—come to find my brother Anthony's got it. Instead of sharing, we'd barter for what the other had. Otherwise, no one was getting anything. Whoever got home first snatched whatever food there was and hid it in their room, or in other places throughout the house. If you didn't, it was likely you didn't eat.

There is no becoming a healthy, positive person with an "every man for himself" mentality. It's just not possible.

We had no one to step into the role of a leader. To say that everyone would eat. That no one had to hide food in order to eat a meal. That should have been my father, but it wasn't.

Dad was supposed to be the moral guy who showed up—who did right by us and helped out however he could. Instead, when he was there, he was a bully. Bullies only agitate and annoy people, rather than ingratiate themselves to them. All his actions did was drive me away from him—drove me to do the opposite of what it was I had the potential to do.

A DIFFERENT PATH

Once I quit the trumpet, I continued to decline. I did a whole bunch of nothing for the four remaining years of high school. I was in the streets more than I was in school. I had no purpose. I developed the mentality that life didn't matter—that I didn't matter, and so *nothing* mattered. I was going to dominate whatever space I was in and I didn't have to explain or justify anything to anyone.

Teachers continued to try to help me—to pull me through. Same with counselors. Whoever they could throw at me. Mr. Duvall, my ninth-grade teacher saw that I was gifted and tried to teach me leadership. He saw that, early on, I was a good influence on other students. He put me in a program to develop my potential. I rock climbed and taught others how to do it as part of his leadership training, and I was good at it—but as with everything else, after too long, I just quit.

I'd show up to class whenever I felt like, sometimes with a friend and his boombox in tow. My friend wasn't even a student in the class, but I did what I wanted, so I brought him with me, regardless. I recall clearly one day when one of the teachers wasn't having it, so she told us to get out. No skin off our nose, so we roamed the hallways, radio playing. Security stopped us in the hall.

"Dre, you have to get out of the hallway. The superintendent is coming."

Though we didn't know the "super," we knew that no one was having any of my bullshit on the days he came to visit. Nobody was tolerating anything because the boss was coming. He told us to go to the gym, but the gangs that ran our neighborhood ran that gym. We had a big-ass radio and no gun to stop them from trying to take it from us.

"Can't go to the gym, dude," I told the security guard.

He told us to head to the auditorium—that there was some kind of meeting for students there, so just go sit in the back and be quiet. He wasn't supposed to let anyone in there, but he had to put us somewhere.

We listened and planted ourselves in the back of the auditorium. There is a black man in a bow tie up front, telling the students about an opportunity for them to go to Italy and China. To Sweden and France. To London. They can travel the world. Of course, I didn't buy a word of it.

I stood up and said, "Yo, this is some bullshit."

"What do you mean?" he asked me.

"You got kids up there with you that don't even go to this school, talking about you going to send us somewhere. You ain't sending nobody nowhere. You full of shit."

Instead of backing down, the man in the bow tie said, "Don't talk from back there. Come talk down here." My friend laughed at my having been called out. I wasn't going to be punked, so I made my way down to the front. It was the first step towards what would be my best and last chance to deviate from the path I was on.

And I blew it.

CHAPTER FOUR

DOUBLING DOWN

It was in my nature to be the best at whatever it was I decided to do. Therefore, if I was going to be a fuck up, I was going to be the best fuck up *ever*.

That man in the black bow tie called me out, not just in front of my boy, but in front of all those honor roll students and other assorted "good" kids in the auditorium. There was no way I was *not* going down to talk to him. President Reagan had created some kind of program where he wanted inner-city kids—aka black kids—to gain some kind of international experience and see parts of the world they'd likely never see otherwise.

The only way to get black kids accepted to this kind of program would be to eliminate grades as part of the requirement. I'm more than positive the powers that be had a meeting where someone said, "We want black kids to go on these trips. How do we get them selected?" Then someone else probably said, "If we make it all about grades, you're not going to get black kids. You'll only get white and Asian kids."

What they came up with was a student exchange program.

They had approximately eighty-four scholarships for the city of Boston, but they would not be awarded on the basis of grades. They would be given based on the potential of the child. People from the exchange committee would have to meet the children and speak with them to determine if they were appropriate.

The man in the black bow tie handed me the forms I needed to fill out and said something that I'll never forget:

> "Don't say 'no' for them," he told me. "Fill out this form. Turn it in. Let *them* tell you no, then you can complain. Don't say 'no' for them without asking."

That should have been enough. He spoke truth and it should have been a slap in my face, telling me to wake up and get my shit together—to let others tell me no before I said no for myself. To stop assuming that I couldn't achieve and give up before I'd even started.

It *should* have been enough. Like I said, the damage had already been done.

Fast forward approximately four months. I'm sitting at home, doing nothing as usual. Suddenly, and without reason, the date the forms were due clicked in my head. I opened a drawer in my room and there sat the forms. I decided to fill them out. A friend, Derek, was hanging out with me. He was a high-school dropout with a stolen car.

"Yo, D," I said. "Give me a ride."

"WHAT'S UP WITH THE RADIO?"

We jumped in his car. I remember we had leather bomber jackets on, carrying that big-ass radio with us again. We pulled up to the front of the school and strolled up to the door, boombox in hand. There was a white woman standing at the front door. She had a pearl necklace. Classic suburban white lady look. This is important because this was Boston in the 1980s. As a young black man, you didn't give white people in Boston a hard time.

"What do you want?" she asked.

"Nothing," I said. I hadn't really thought through what I'd say. I didn't expect to run into anyone at the door.

"No," she said. "What do you want?"

"We're here for the student exchange program," I told her.

She asked for the application and looked it over. Then she asked me where my essay was. I told her I didn't have one, and she responded that it was mandatory to have an essay in order to complete the application.

"Okay, I don't have an essay," I said. "I'm gone."

I turned to leave, and she stopped me. She told me to sit down right where I was. She gave me a piece of paper and a pencil and she told me to write my essay there on the spot.

I don't know why, but I did it. Maybe it was because I didn't want trouble with this white woman. Maybe it was because there was a part of me that hadn't given up completely. Either way, I wrote that essay and gave it to her.

We had been sitting on the floor of the hallway, and she let us into this large conference room of the school, full of parents. There were tables lined up everywhere, all manned by the different student exchange programs. There were kids and their families, moms and dads, sisters and brothers, sometimes even grandma and grandpa, and everyone is dressed up. They're all going from table to table, interviewing.

There were thirty-five companies offering eighty-four scholarships. Company "A" would interview thirty kids, and at the end of those interviews, they would make a list—almost like a draft order. It would be a list of their top ten if they could get anyone they wanted. If a certain kid on that list had a good application, then they would take that child. All of the other companies there worked in a similar way. In this way, it was possible that you could be a kid that no one wanted.

I went from table to table and I interviewed—me and my high school dropout friend in our leather bombers, carrying a huge radio, looking at all of the white and Asian families who were dressed to the nines. I hit all the tables, thinking not one of these companies was going to be interested in me, and we left.

On the way out, someone asked, "What's up with the radio?"

"We dance," I told them. Then we showed them.

We hit the hallway, turned on that box, and we broke it down. I mean we literally started break dancing in the hall. What seemed like the entire building came out into the hall and watched us do our routine. When we were done, we grabbed our radio and we went home.

The next month, I got a call from the award committee.

I won the first scholarship out of eighty-four kids. That meant I was number one on everyone's list.

One company was an exchange student program that only went to the south of France. They called me and told me that they wanted to take me, but that one of their prerequisites was that I had to speak French to come to their program. Despite that, they were trying to find a way around it because they wanted me that badly.

Number one on every list. For the year 1984, I had the most potential of any high school kid in the city of Boston. Of all people, I was awarded the scholarship. Three years of flunking. Assaulting my senior class president. I was nothing but a fuck up and I had just won a student exchange scholarship from the president.

My headmaster, Mr. Hennessy, received the letter. It said,

"Andre Norman: Scholarship Winner."

This, of course, drove him bananas. He called me into the office and flipped out. He went so far as to bring the man in the black bow tie to the school for a meeting with the three of us. The principal told him that under no circumstances was I going to represent their school—that I was flunking, that I was a bad kid, and that I was a criminal. The man in the black bow tie listened, and when Mr. Hennessy had finished, he calmly said,

> "One, it's not your money. Two, it's not your call. Three, he is going."

> Then he looked at me and said again, "Never say 'no' for them. You're going."

It was the first time anyone had ever stood up for me. Ever. A white principal screaming at me—with cause, no less— and this man let him say all those true things about me and still said, "he's going." I couldn't believe it.

A NEW HUSTLE

So now I've got the scholarship. I went to an awards ceremony to receive it, an event my mother attended. I don't think she knew what it was about or what it was for, or had any idea that this scholarship meant that I was going to Europe. At sixteen, I was going on my first world tour. Step one, I had to pick a company. One offered me a five-country tour.

"I'll take that one," I said.

Next, I needed a passport. Clothes. Soap. This, that, and the other thing. All items I didn't have—nothing that I needed for traveling out of the country. I had to find a way to get it.

I had an older cousin who came to visit from time to time. He was a drug addict, and he often took me out with him. He lived in the suburbs, but he would come down to see me in the city. "Dre, show me around," he'd tell me. We'd go out driving and he'd see someone on the sidewalk. He'd tell me to stop the car, and he'd jump out and mug them. He'd then jump back in the car and tell me to drive off. He'd do it a few more times in the same night.

I learned a new hustle. Now I needed money to get these things for my trip. And I knew just how to get it.

I got a couple of my friends together and headed out to the suburbs and we straight-up robbed people. My parents were able to cover the passport, so my objective was to get enough money for clothes and a suitcase. I didn't even have that to my name—what was a kid like me going to do with a suitcase? Where was I going?

Jail. That's where.

In all my robbing and stealing, I eventually got caught, like most people do. We were arrested in the middle of May, approximately thirty days before my birthday. Any later and I would have been tried as an adult, which would have been a whole different set of circumstances for me.

We went to court and my mother was there. The judge, a black woman, called me to stand and began reading off the charges. I felt my face turning blue, because I wasn't breathing. I saw my mother's face turning colors, too.

And then fate intervened.

During a short recess, someone told the judge that I had been awarded a scholarship to go to Europe. They asked for a continuance, to push the case until September to allow me to go on the trip.

Now I don't know what this judge was thinking. Maybe she saw another young black man about to end up in the system with the opportunity to take a different path. Considering my record, she had every reason to say, "No, he blew it."

She didn't.

She granted us the continuance and moved the hearing to the necessary date, allowing me to take the trip. I returned home and bought a couple of outfits—I distinctly remember having a gray one and a brown one. My father, of all people, drove me to the airport in a car full of his friends, in yet another car I didn't recognize. He dropped me off at Boston Logan Airport. I don't remember a thing he said to me. At that point in my life, his voice sounded to me like Charlie Brown's teacher—completely unintelligible, in one ear and out the other.

None of that mattered, though. I was going to Europe. Once there, it was an incredible time. I met my best friend, Morgan, a young Jewish girl out of Miami. I was the only "inner city"—read black—kid on the tour. Everyone else was from these super-rich suburbs that I'd never heard of. Their parents paid tens of thousands of dollars for them to be on the trip.

I met kids I would have never met running the streets in Boston. I met one kid whose grandfather owned a department store in Massachusetts—one where I had been caught shoplifting before. When the kid and I met, I said, "Man, I owe you all some money."

It was wild. Here I was with all of these super-elite kids, and none of them had never met a city black kid before. When they met up with me, you would have thought they lost their minds. Everyone saw me as different, but not in a bad way. They thought I was cool. Everyone wanted to hang out with Dre. I spent the whole summer being cool—with *everybody*. It was a feeling I'd never known before.

At one point, I started getting questions about whether or not my parents were coming to the end-of-season recital. I didn't understand. How were my parents—how were anyone's parents—going to make a trip to Europe just for some recital to close out the tour?

Sure enough, all the other kids' parents showed up for it. I felt embarrassed and left out, but then something crazy happened—all the kids wanted their parents to meet me. I must have gone to four or five different dinners and lunches. One of the kids' fathers had a castle over there that I got to visit. I'd never experienced anything like it— and it didn't stop there.

That summer, the musical *Cats* was running. Almost all of the events on the European tour were free, but things like that cost more money. One of the girls on the trip, Christina, knew I didn't have the money and gave me her ticket. I went to see it, and I cried. I had never seen a musical, and it was one of the most touching things I had ever seen.

There was a local pub in London that we would visit frequently. There was one of those old stand-up video game cabinets—this was 1984, remember—and I was the video game king. I would get a high score every time I played. When you did that, you could put in three letters as your initials or your name. I always used to put D-R-E. Before too long, the entire leaderboard said "Dre."

Then I realized, I wasn't Dre there. I was the American. Being the American meant I was the same as the white kids. The people there didn't see us in terms of color—just what country we came from. I had never been seen as equal to any white kids. I didn't want to be white, but I was never confused with white kids where I came from. The idea that I was seen on equal footing with white kids there was just incredible to me.

The leaderboard on the video game read U-S-A all the way down by the time I left.

EVERYBODY LOVES DRE

As I said, all the kids loved being on the trip with me. When they went home, apparently, they were telling their parents all about me, telling them that they want to go again next year, and they have to be on the same trip that Dre is on. The company received calls from almost all of the kid's parents, requesting their kids be on whichever trip I was supposed to be on next time.

The company called me and brought me back down to their office.

"Here's what we're going to do, Dre," they told me. "Last year, the president paid for you to go on that trip. Next year, *we're* going to pay for you to go. We'll pick the trip and we're going to send you on it. If that goes as well as last year went, we're going to make you a junior counselor."

At that age, even with as amazing an offer as that was, I had no grasp of how huge this offer was—so my response was, "Cool. That works." That summer, I turned eighteen years old. I was all set to go on the trip. I had my passport. Everything was in place for me to have the summer of my life, all expenses paid, taking a step toward a new life.

Then, about three weeks before I was supposed to leave, I got on a bus and went to New York. No reason. I just wanted to go. I had no concept of what I was walking away from.

Instead of going back to Europe and becoming an international youth counselor, I went to New York to hang out with friends who were no good for me and got myself right back into trouble. The trip came and went. After too long, I ended up back in Boston, and that's when the wheels really came off. I went back to robbing and stealing. Running around with a shotgun and .357 Magnum. Robbing drug houses. Completely wilding out.

Europe was a cliff, and not going was my taking the leap from the edge. It was the last stop. There was no going back. I didn't have the sense to know what I was giving up. There was no one in my life to provide me with the structure to carry me through, because I had no one to share it with—at least not anyone capable of celebrating it with me, because they didn't care.

There was no fanfare. No one to celebrate Dre, the exchange student. I might as well have told the people in my life that I was going to summer camp, or that I was headed out to the mall. Telling them I was going to Europe had the exact same effect. I took the trip and came back. Nothing changed. Nobody cared. Nobody said anything. I won this prestigious award, and, just like always, I was alone with it.

It would have been ten times better if my family had celebrated with me. It would have been one hundred times better if my mom and dad had said to themselves that they would put together whatever money it took to make sure I had what I needed to take the trip. Maybe I wouldn't have felt like I had to rob people to buy the things I needed.

So, it was on me to make the best decision for myself, and I was the last person that should have been responsible for my own well-being. I told myself that if nobody else gave a damn about it, then I shouldn't, either. Europe was the last station on the tracks for me and I blew right through it.

The next stop was prison.

CLIMBING THE LADDER ALL THE WAY DOWN

I got sent to the county jail, and while in there, I decided to beat down the toughest guy there. I succeeded, and that got me sent to a different county jail. I used the same strategy and fought the toughest guy there, along with the staff and other inmates. That got me kicked out and sent to another county jail. I strong-armed that place as well and ended up, quite literally, taking it over. I physically dominated the entire facility and did whatever I wanted to do—just like my father had shown me by his example.

Then I got sentenced to state prison—and that scared me to death. Now I was actually in over my head. I had no idea what to do with those circumstances, and I was just as scared about not knowing as I was about being in prison. Fear is a hell of a motivator, though it doesn't always motivate someone to make the best decisions. I decided that I was going to fuck up the first dude that came near me.

The first guy that walked up to me turned out to be one of my best friends from the dummy class—way back in the third grade. It turned out that entire prison was filled with people from the dummy class, kids from the special needs classes, from the principal's office, from juvenile probation; people who quit football, quit band.

It was a building full of quitters.

Lucky for me, Dominic from the neighborhood was still in there when I arrived.

I came out of "new-man" and there was Dominic, my childhood hero, to greet me. I would have done *anything* to hang out with him back in the day. Here all I had to do was rob a few people. If I had known that, I would have been in there a long time ago. As scared as I was, getting to hang out with Dominic was a dream come true.

When you first get sentenced, they send you to maximum-security. You might stay there for three to four days, after which they'll send you to the classification center. Then they essentially send you to an appropriate institution, wherever that was. I stayed at the max for about four days, which meant four days of hanging out with Dominic. When it came time for me to go to the classification center, I needed to know what it took to go back to where Dominic was. They looked at my sentence and said that I was likely going to a low-level medium-security prison.

"That's good for you," they told me.

No, it's not, I thought. That's not where Dominic would be. Dominic was at the max, Walpole. The person in the classification office told me that people typically ended up in Walpole if they caused trouble. That was all I needed to hear. I beat up everybody I could get my hands on—

cussed out every correctional officer. After two weeks of that, they sent me back to max with Dominic.

Dominic had a natural life sentence, and the inner circle of his gang all had life sentences as well. When he brought me into the gang, I had no idea I was surrounded by lifers. Not realizing this, I began to take on their personalities. I saw things the way they saw things. Processed them the way they did. Did things the way they did.

Because I was new, I was on the bottom rung. Surprisingly, you can see a lot from the bottom. I saw their power. I saw their influence. State maximum-security prison is the ultimate arena to be in if you want to be a tough guy—and I wanted to be on that top rung. Dominic was number one and I was chasing that goal. He was my guidepost.

Over the next six years, I destroyed anything and everything in my way, until I went from number twenty thousand in the prison system to number three.

CHAPTER FIVE

THE KING OF NOWHERE

To become the number one gang leader in the Massachusetts prison system, I had to get a body—a murder within the prison walls.

I was going to get seven of them.

I'd been placed back in state prison, having earned my stripes during my four-year quest. I ran it with an iron fist. I had gotten into an altercation with a younger gang and picked up two attempted murder charges, which added another ten years to my sentence. This earned me two years in solitary confinement from the general prison population. That means twenty-four hours a day, locked in a cell by myself. I was on "10 Block," the worst housing unit for the most dangerous criminals in the state of Massachusetts. It holds sixty people. I was one of the worst of the worst, and so I had become a routine "visitor."

If you're on 10 Block, you've tried to kill someone, you've tried to escape, or you've committed some other kind of horrendous act to end up there. Time there is a sentence within a sentence—whatever your actual sentence might be is secondary to your being placed on 10 Block. A hearing board determines if you go there and for how long, depending on what you've done.

I was sent there for stabbing a number of other prisoners.

My mother came to visit me while I was in segregation for stabbing those prisoners. She was tired. She'd been yelling at me for being crazy for years. Meanwhile, I thought I was winning. You couldn't tell me anything. I was ranking. I was moving up in the world. I established myself. I'm the number three guy. I'm telling myself this is the best thing ever.

My mother looked at me and asked me:

"How do you get in jail, in jail?"

She realized she had lost her son. "This is some strange man who took over his body," she said. She said goodbye, gave me a hug, and she left—but she left crying. She knew I had gone off the deep end. I wasn't her kid. I wasn't the trumpet player. In her mind, I was lost.

The system got her kid.

There were strict rules and protocols for every action on 10 Block. One of those was that if we were to move anywhere, because of the danger we presented—even to the guards—we were to be in handcuffs and shackles with two escorts. One day, for whatever reason, there was a skeleton crew of guards working, and a rookie was handling my movement from the library. He didn't have his secondary partner and didn't know what he was doing.

He opened the door and told me to come with him. No second escort. No cuffs.

I figured it was a setup—that there were eight correctional officers around the corner waiting to hand me a beating. Still, I followed him—on point—down the stairs. Nothing happened. When we reached my tier, it dawned on him that he couldn't lock me in and close the door to the unit at the same time, so he locked me on the tier, but not in my cell.

As you can imagine, this did not sit well with the lieutenant. He called them to let them know I was loose on the tier, and they panicked. The head of the unit ran to the door and asked me what I was doing, wanting to keep me calm. At this point, inmates in other cells could have handed me a knife, or any other kind of weapon. Getting me back in my cell, in their minds, was going to be a violent proposition.

I had other ideas.

Getting me to my cell was going to be the easy part. Their having to write up that one of the most dangerous men in the prison was walking around a maximum restraint block unrestrained? That posed a bigger problem for them.

If the higher-ups found out about me being on the block free of shackles and cuffs, they would have had to admit to a complete breakdown in protocol in their report. There would have been hell to pay from their superiors. People lost their jobs over those kinds of incidents—incidents that were supposed to be unheard of.

The lieutenant later visited me in my cell and asked me how I was feeling. I said, "You know something? When you guys put me back in my cell, I kind of hurt my back. I think I need to go to the hospital. If I have to go to the hospital, they are going to ask for the use of force report that will explain how you had to drag me down the tier unrestrained."

"What would make your back feel better?" he asked me.

"Going to 9 Block," I responded.

The environment in 9 Block was a step down from 10

Block. There were more privileges, more movement, and less overall hostility. It was a place where people wanted to be less aggressive, or somewhere they sent prisoners who had earned favor with the guards. Guys like me didn't go to 9 Block. The lieutenant knew that and so did I—but there we were.

"So if I send you to 9 block you won't need to go to the hospital?" the lieutenant asked me.

"I'll sleep like a baby," I said. I gave him the "I win" smirk and saluted. "Yes, sir."

I was on 9 Block by the time lunch ended.

AN UNWELCOME TRANSITION

Once there, everything was relatively cool. There was an "Andre's in charge" moment where I had to "inform" the guy who thought *he* was in charge that that was not the case. Other than that, there were no other fights. No drama, no problems. Life, for all intents and purposes, was good. Before I knew it, I was three months away from being returned to the prison's general population.

Then one day, a guard tells me that I'm needed downstairs. They put me in cuffs and shackles and took me to see the lieutenant.

The lieutenant informed me that I was being shipped to MCI-Norfolk for a transition program. It's an intensive program—typical of the television shows you've seen when they get in your face and yell and scream at you—and at the end of six months, you're let out of segregation, no matter how long your sentence was prior to going in. You don't get selected for this program. You have to apply. Yet here I was, not only being chosen, but being told I *had* to go.

For any other inmate, this would have been welcome news. Six months and then freedom? That's a no-brainer. Problem was, I only had *three* months left before I was sent back to general population. Instead of getting out of segregation, I was getting a three-month extension.

I was not pleased. They just added three months. That was in no way worth it to me. They returned me to my cell, packed up my things, and put me in the van. When I arrived, they brought me in for the interview. They fed me the standard bullshit that they give to everyone. I stopped them mid-speech.

"Listen, let me explain something to you," I said. "I don't want to be here. I *shouldn't* be here. I didn't *ask* to come here. I was fucking kidnapped. I have no beef with any of your staff. My beef is with the staff back at maximum-security. I'm going to do your six months, and when I'm done, I'm going to go back there and I'm going to take it out on them, so let's make this real simple. Don't none of you talk to me, and I won't talk to you. Easy. If I ain't got it coming, I don't want it. If it ain't mine, don't ask me. That's it. Now take me to my fucking cell."

After that, I didn't speak. Silence, I knew, was the biggest weapon of them all. They took me to my cell, and I laid down. I talked to no one. Did my three meals a day, three showers a week, recreation four times a week—but I never spoke. After about a week of my self-imposed silence, people started to get uneasy, especially considering the reputation that preceded me.

The upside to being there was that I got more movements there, which meant instead of eating in my cell, there was a small cafeteria where everybody came to eat. I got recreational time without handcuffs and shackles in a big yard instead of the dog kennel I had before. Still, I did no work and I spoke to no one. I bided my time.

Three months in and I still was silent as a monk. I'd begun talking to the other prisoners during rec time, but never to the guards, which of course, drove them crazy. Otherwise, I was good. No fights. No issues. Whatever their game had been in sending me there, I wasn't playing. I was going to do the time they'd given me and go back to general population.

Then a pivotal moment in my life presented itself.

TIME TO TAKE MY THRONE

I heard a call from a cell in the tier above me. It was Willie Manor, a prisoner I knew from my time in maximum-security at Walpole.

"Yo, Dre," he said. "You know there was a riot yesterday at the max and all your guys got stabbed up."

The riot had been between the white and black gangs. Our side won in the end, but things went badly in the beginning, and a lot of my guys were in bad shape.

Of course, when I heard this, I had nothing but retaliation on my mind. I did the math. I was ready. There were white guys on my unit. My plan was to get my team together and attack those white guys. Mind you, one of them had become a close friend. We played basketball together every day—he had the jump shot, I had the post game. In fact, he was waiting on the court for me at that moment.

But a line had been drawn. The white guys had attacked the black guys, so I had to take out the white guys. It didn't matter that my friend was one of them. As soon as Willie finished telling me the story, I was going to round up a crew and attack as many of the white guys as I could. I was going to get that body and then some.

To murder someone—not on the streets, but in prison—earns you the ultimate respect. I ended up in solitary confinement for two attempted murders inside. I was kicked out of federal prisons for trying to get a body. If I was able to pull this off, not only would I have achieved that respect, but I would have initiated a war. Starting a war in prison gets that war named after you. I'd been fighting for over six years to become the number one guy. It wasn't about the time I put in—it was the work. Now here was my chance to jump the line—gift wrapped like a Christmas present. I would be a legend.

I would be the king.

Then God spoke to me.

"WHAT AM I SUPPOSED TO DO?"

I stood there in the yard. All of us were listening to Willie's story. I was prepared to lead my mob down the ramp and attack these men. I was thinking about the legendary status this war would bring me. I was actually happy Willie was telling me this story, and I was chomping at the bit for him to finish. He did.

Just then, God said, "Don't do it, life choice."

I can't tell you how I know it was God. When you know, you know. I knew it was him—and it made me angry. Furious, really.

"Why are you speaking to me?" I asked him. "All my life, you've never been there."

My mother used to get beat down to the floor every day by my father. Where was God? The white kids used to throw rocks at us and call us niggers on the bus. Where was God? When my dad walked out of the house and didn't come back, where was God? They put me in a dummy class because I didn't read and write. God never showed up. Every Saturday, I sat at home wishing my dad would take me to the park. God didn't show up. He didn't show up, just like my father didn't, when I sat alone at my graduation, embarrassed beyond measure. He didn't show up when I went to school with dirty clothes, relentlessly mocked by the other kids.

"You don't know me," I told him. "You've been showing up for everyone but me all this time. I'm not on Your list. There're people in some church crying hallelujah with their faces to the floor, but I'm not on that team. *I* run this shit, and when I do this thing, I'll run it all. I don't need you or your advice."

Again, He said, "Don't do it, life choice." No matter how hard I pushed back, He said it over and over again.

"Okay, then," I finally said to him. "What am I supposed to do?"

When I was sent to prison, it was like returning a fish to water. No adjustment periods—nothing to get used to. I didn't care where they put me. It didn't matter how much time they gave me. It didn't matter how much they tried to torture me or how much they tried to take from me. I came from nothing—what could they take? Nothing that mattered. As long as they couldn't separate me from me, there was no way they could win—no way they could ever defeat me.

So, there I was, physically locked in the yard. The white guys I had every intention of attacking were to my left. The gate to the yard is on the right, guarded by the CO. Beyond that, I was a gang member—a gang leader. I hurt people—it's what I did. I'm now in the position to hurt a lot of people and I have no way out of this yard. How am I supposed to not do this thing that I seem meant to do?

With no word from anyone, the CO put his key in the gate and opened it.

I had two options. My chance at being number one was

to my left. The open gate was to my right. Nobody knew what I was about to do, least of all the CO. I hadn't said any of my intentions out loud. I stood in the middle of that yard with a choice—and I made it.

I walked out that gate.

The CO locked it behind me. I walked back into the main hallway, walked down to my cell, stepped in, and they locked the door.

THE EPIPHANY

There were no visions. I didn't start speaking in tongues. I sat in my prison cell, with my state blanket and the knife I always had with me—and I realized it was over. I realized that everything I had done up until that point was another life, and it was now behind me. All that I had done had made me a king—but I had become a king of nowhere.

My whole world came to the proverbial screeching halt. I compare it now to Michael Jordan just after his retirement press conference. What does the greatest basketball player on the planet do when he decides to hang it up before his prime is over? The world around him didn't understand it. I was the Michael Jordan of prison. No one was going to understand why I would just quit the path that I was on. Why, when you were so close to having everything you ever wanted?

Just like for Mike, it was time—but it wasn't easy.

It was like being in a car wreck. You've just been smashed to bits, the airbags have deployed, and you sit in there in shock for what feels like forever. Time slows down. The walk back to my cell felt like miles, the time sitting there alone like years. I had to accept that God had blocked the path to becoming the number one psychopath in prison. When I did, just like that, my goal of being the king was gone—but if I couldn't be a psychopath, what could I be? What was it that I actually wanted for myself? I sat in my cell the rest of that day, by myself, working that out.

It hurt me that my friends were attacked, but I had to let go of retaliating. I let every little piece of that life go. Everything I've done in my life, I've done with intention. When I made a decision, I went with it. If I was going to rob a place, I was never 98 percent there on the idea. If I was going to stab a man in the yard, there wasn't a 1 percent chance it wouldn't happen. God showed me the path, and I decided to take it—along with something else.

I decided I wanted to change.

So, in my mind, I looked at everyone who was in prison with me. The white guys, the black guys, the Spanish guys, the Asian guys, the snitches, the church guys, the Muslims, the fake Muslims, the fake Christians, the guys who work in the kitchen, the guys who play ball, the guys who play chess, the guys who clean up, the psychopaths, the guys on meds—out of all of them, none of them went home and did good. They all came back, and they brought friends.

It was then that I realized: Freedom doesn't work. Freedom is a trick. Most people got free and came back. What I had to become was successful. As a rule, successful people didn't end up where I was. Being successful, to me, meant going to college. I chose Harvard University, not because it was the number one university in the world, but because it was close to my house and I used to ride my skateboard there as a kid. It was also the only school I knew the name of. Once I'd made that decision, I knew what I had to do next.

Like Michael Jordan, I had to have my press conference.

The next day, I came out of my cell and I gathered up my guys. They were looking for me to rally them up and get them ready for the retaliation they knew had to be coming.

"Listen," I told them. "This is the plan. I'm going home. I'm going to Harvard. I'm going to be successful."

The looks on their faces are what I imagined Phil Jackson's face looked like when Jordan dropped the retirement news on him.

"What are you talking about?" they said. "This is what you do. You're a gang leader. You're a criminal. You're a psychopath. You don't do anything else."

I told them: I'm going home. I'm going to Harvard. I'm going to be successful.

Still they told me I couldn't. You're black, they said. You're a gang leader. You don't read that well. You're in the hole for trying to kill eight people. You're a psychopath. You're doing an eighteen- to twenty-five-year bid.

Had I known the scriptures like I know them today, I'd have said, "Satan, get behind me." Instead, I told them, "Yo, get out of my way."

This wasn't a group decision, I told them. No one was telling them *they* had to quit. They could continue to do their thing and I wouldn't be mad at them—but I was out of there. I knew with absolute clarity that my thinking about everything in life had been wrong. I had been living a lie, but I had convinced myself that everything was as it should be—so much so that I didn't see the lie.

When I did, I had to separate myself from the emotions of it. If I hadn't been able to do that, I might never have gotten out—especially because, as I sat in that cell, there were parts of me that wanted to stay. Parts of me that said, "This works. You've accomplished something. Don't leave what we've done. We've conditioned ourselves to this space and we're not only good at this, we're *great* at this."

The parts of me that listened to God spoke louder. Those parts said, "This is over." That began a struggle, an internal battle between the thing I was good at and the unknown. I didn't know if I was going to finish. I made it in prison, but I didn't know if I could make it on the outside. More powerful than the fear of that unknown, though, was the challenge. That alone tipped the scale. Before that moment, I had challenged myself to be Andre the Invincible, but no more. Going from number 20,000 in the prison system, to number three, to the doorstep of number one had been an impossible challenge and I had done it. Now I had the chance to do the impossible again.

Sitting in that cell, I thought of all the teachers who had shown me love:

Ms. Oliver, Mr. McDonald, Mrs. Ellis, Mr. Solis, Mrs. Henderson, Mr. Bevilacqua. Mr. Duvall, Mr. Gill, Mrs. Morrison.

All these teachers used to tell me how smart I was, how gifted I was, how brave I was—and I started hearing their voices. I heard what they used to say to me versus what others had said to me, about how I wasn't going to be shit; how my homies used to say we weren't ever going to amount to anything; how the police told me I'd never be anybody.

My teachers' words and encouragement became a shield around me, as I marched in the opposite direction of where I had been going, of the world I had been living in. They helped me forge my way through.

I've seen many a people come before me who had their epiphany moment, tried to act on it, and got blown back into the pile because they didn't have anything to hold on to. I held onto their words until the end.

But first, I was going to need a plan.

CHAPTER SIX

LEARNING TO WALK

A HARD BUT NECESSARY DECISION

So many people wake up and say, "I'm not going to drink anymore." They wake up and say, "I'm not going to use drugs anymore." They're not going to gamble anymore. They're not going to cheat on their taxes anymore. They say it definitively, as though speaking it into existence will make it happen.

Willpower alone doesn't work.

They walk back into a room full of thieves. Full of drinkers, addicts, liars, and cheats. They stand in the bathroom of the bar, still telling themselves they won't drink, then let their friends convince them to have one more when they return to them.

It's not to say that their moment of clarity isn't real—at least not to them. They've convinced themselves of their own lie. They truly feel that they want to stop doing these things, yet they continue to surround themselves with people who are actively bringing them down.

They can have that moment—that epiphany—fifty times in a week, and it will be meaningless each time. Unless there is a plan to fulfill that epiphany and make it stick, there is no point. Thoughts are deceiving. Thoughts can be manipulated. Once it's written down, an idea is given power.

Remember the last time you tried to go on a diet? Which number attempt was that? How many times did you find yourself sitting in McDonald's after you just downed a Big Mac, telling yourself that was the last one? You felt terrible afterwards. You tell yourself you're going to die, that you're not going to see your kids grow up, and that you're going to Subway from now on.

Unless you create a plan, you'll find yourself wiping that special sauce off your face again. You have to find the gym and join. You have to get the workout clothes you need. You have to plan your meals. Then you have to do it over and over again until you'll go to the gym no matter what you're wearing. Until eating anything but healthy is no longer an option. There's a lot of things that must simply go out the door. It's the byproduct of making a hard but necessary decision to improve your life.

When I told my crew I was leaving, their first response was, "No."

I repeated to them that I was going to Harvard and I was going to be successful. They wanted to laugh at me, but I had a habit of stabbing people, so they kept that to themselves. My best friend, though—my top guy—pulled me aside and gave me all the reasons why I couldn't go.

When I was in the ninth grade, my friends gave me all the reasons I couldn't play the trumpet. When my top man was giving me all the reasons why I couldn't go to Harvard, he sounded just like those high school friends, and I came to a realization:

> "You won't steal my dream again," I told him. "I kept friends like you last time and that's how I ended up here."

In all honesty, him saying the same thing I heard in ninth grade was the best thing he could have done for me. It made me see that not only did I need a new goal, but I needed a new setting. Those exact words coming out of his mouth so many years later hit me with a huge sense of déjà vu—as well as a sense of purpose. I needed to walk it and live it to show people where I stood and what I stood for. I had to stay away from what these people were doing as much as I could while I tried to achieve this goal.

Not an easy feat in a confined space like prison.

When I got back to gen pop, I ate in the cafeteria. Tables wound all the way across. I had three tables in the middle as I had the biggest gang—almost forty men. I sat in between the two other tables, in the center seat. The Irish had their tables. Same with the Italians. Spanish guys. Everyone had their tables and based on your prison ranking or your gang status, you knew who everyone was based on where they sat. If someone wasn't a member of a gang or wasn't recognized by one, they ate standing over a trash can. My very first day in the cafeteria, I tried to sit at the white table because I knew one of them—he was my cellmate in county lockup. I saw him and he told me—with just a look—"Man, I love you, but this ain't going to happen." Luckily, Dominic saw me and brought me to his table. The rest, as they say, was history.

I left my table.

Part of my new plan was to be honest with myself—to shed myself of the collateral stuff. The central stuff? That was easy. I'm going to be honest and open. Then I started to ask myself: what does that really mean? It meant I had to make the adjustments. There were certain things I just wasn't going to be able to do anymore, or things I would need to do. It couldn't be superficial, because superficial wouldn't work. That was going to be the hardest part.

My guys were all against me—well, against the concept. The fear of me didn't change with my decision to leave, so no one was bold enough to go against me directly, though I know they all wanted to laugh at me. My mother did when I called her to tell her. My grandmother thought I had lost my mind.

I called my father.

He told me, "We're not that type of people. We can't be that. That Harvard shit is crazy talk. You can't do that." My father grew up in Virginia in the 1940s. Black wasn't welcome on certain streets. Black couldn't walk across certain boulevards. We were "boys," not men. We couldn't be born in a hospital—my father was born in his own home. When I told him I was going to a private, essentially white institution, he said, "They're not going to let you." His "they" were the whites from 40s Virginia. He then called me an asshole and hung up the phone. It was the first time I heard fear in my dad's voice. It didn't excuse the years of him being an awful father, but I connected with him on a certain level, because I knew what it was like to be scared.

All my father knew was how to run from me. He couldn't

embrace my plan, so he ran. That's when I realized that in making this decision, I was alone again. I told myself to embrace it. Alone has worked for you, I told myself. You can do it alone. I'd been alone forever. I was used to it. It also made me realize that my vision was for me—that I was sharing it with all the wrong people, people who didn't respect or acknowledge what I was trying to do. I tried to share it with gang members and psychopaths, and the men who create psychopaths, how I'm going to do this thing they've never done. They simply couldn't understand it. However, I reached out to Dominic, my OG, and he cosigned—he told me to go for it.

It was only natural to want to share it with them. They were the closest to friends I had. Who else was I going to share it with? It was hard for me to realize that I couldn't run to the people who weren't living—who had maybe never lived—in my headspace. I had to remind myself that the decision was for me. Once I could do that, I could focus on my "why." Once I found myself, I had to create a plan, and in creating a plan, I would seek to find my tribe—those would understand my goal and encourage and support me in the ways I needed to succeed.

The biggest favor those who rejected my idea could have done for me was to not believe me. Had they not, I would have tried to bring them on my journey. That would have been catastrophic.

That's where so many others who only focused on freedom failed. They brought their saboteurs with them. Then they do what they do—sabotage—and the people that brought them with them stand asking themselves, "What happened?" when they should have known better. Those people got them where they were—why did they ever think that bringing them with them would change their circumstances?

I knew that in order to make this happen, I needed to get settled first. I had to deal with me. I had to love my idea, and by extension, love myself. Without that attitude, I was doomed to failure. No one was going to do the work for me.

The plan in some ways was simple: do the opposite of what everyone else around me was doing. Faced with the fact that I had never done something like this before, the only logical plan to me was to flip the script. I had no scientific facts to base this strategy on, but I was going to see that philosophy as step one of the plan.

The more I walked that path, the more alone I became— proof positive that I was going the right way. Going that way and staying that way was easy, but it was difficult to watch all the people I had come to care about inside continuing to go the wrong way. Once you find yourself in that space where things are going well for you, it's hard to watch others do harm to themselves. You want to bring them with you—but you know you can't. The truth is everyone in a sense has agreed to play their role. They decided that the lifestyle they chose was a good thing, or that their attitude about life is a good thing. I understood it because I had done that for most of my life up until that point—but no more. I had a new role to play.

ANGRY BLACK MAN CLASS

I signed up for school as soon as I was able and got my GED. When I finished my GED, I still ended up bounced around a bunch of different prisons. Even though I had this new plan, I still had the reputation I had created for myself, and no prison wanted anything to do with me. I ended up back in max.

Undeterred, I signed up with Mount Wachusett, the local college that came to the prison. My first semester, I took Western Civilization and a math class. I earned a "B" in both classes. Right after that, they took away the Pell Grants I had used to take the classes. Someone decided prisoners shouldn't have free access to college classes. I wasn't about to let that stop me. I began going to the law library and taught myself the law—so much so that I became a jailhouse lawyer. I retained attorneys of my own and together we attacked my cases. We succeeded and I flipped one, winning an appeal and taking ten years off my sentence. My hunger for knowledge and growth grew. I wanted to find the perfect class for me—one that would help me keep the momentum I had built.

I wanted to find a class for the angry black man.

At the time, there were 1.3 million black people incarcerated in the prison system. There *had* to be an angry black man class. Of course, it didn't exist. I asked why, and no one seemed to understand the need for a class that spoke to the anger that black men in prison felt—about how to deal with the systematic racism that funneled them into the system, and how to deal with the atrocities they experienced there, particularly if they're looking to make change the way I was. No one could help me—at least, not at first.

A friend of mine, Gordon Haas, took me to an Alcoholics Anonymous meeting, despite my protests that I didn't drink. He told me to sit down and shut up. He went up and introduced himself as an alcoholic, then introduced me as someone new to the group. Then he hit me with an incredible piece of wisdom.

"Substitute the alcohol for anger," he said. "Any time you hear about how to deal with an alcohol problem, apply that to your anger."

Then he took me to NA, where I substituted heroin for

anger. He took me to Big Book. Twelve Steps. All the various self-help programs. Every time substituting their issues for my own. I had to make do with what I had, and it worked extremely well.

During this time, I had to continue to distance myself from the hustle and game that would bring me down. It was exceedingly hard to do that living in a locked facility, especially when you have a reputation. It was hard for me to dissociate myself from the person I had made myself to the rest of the world. No one remembers Michael Jordan as a baseball player. When he went to play baseball, people brought him basketball memorabilia to sign. Here I was, the guy who had pulled himself off the lead gang table in the cafeteria, going to college. I found myself a little table off to the side, took three soldiers, and I moved to do my own thing.

I had to let the entire prison know that I meant what I said. Someone else was sitting in the lead chair now. Somebody else was running shit. So, I moved the furthest away from it that I could without getting myself chopped up and stuffed into a footlocker. I picked the number two guy and let him become the number one, yet in any facility I was in, I was still recognized as a shot caller. If the president isn't around, but the vice president is, he's the boss. I gave the guy under me all of my connections, gave up most of my money, and I told him I'd be his advisor.

If I walked away completely, I became a threat. I advised him on his operations while I focused on mine. It was the best and safest solution I could come up with. I went to school. I went to the law library. I went to my programs. I did whatever I had to do to stay out of trouble. Then some riots occurred—ones that had nothing to do with me. No matter what, when these things happen, the prisons will ship the leadership out to other facilities. This time around, instead of another max, they sent me to medium-security prison. When this had happened in the past, I'd look to go back to max, because that's where I felt most comfortable.

Not this time. This time, I said, "I'm not going back." They let me stay once they'd seen I was starting to do good work. Instead of starting beefs, I was mediating them. I gave my first speech in that prison—a prison in which I had threatened to kill the warden approximately four years before. When I got there this time, everyone was looking for that guy. Looking for Andre the Invincible. That wasn't me, though. Instead of hanging in the yard, I was in school every day. I was working on what would eventually become this book.

1:00 P.M.

One day, I noticed all the classrooms were empty. I asked the teacher why no one was there. She responded that no one ever signed up. "You want people in school?" I asked her. She said yes. I walked down the hall to talk to the principal and asked him the same question. He agreed that it would be a great thing to have more students in the school. I walked right out of his office and down to the New Man block.

I grabbed a microphone off a desk in New Man and asked who in there didn't have a GED. If they didn't, I wanted them to come down to the desk. Over fifty men came to me. I told the CO to take down all their names, because they were going to school with me at 1:00 p.m. that day. I wanted him to write them a pass and that was it. He agreed.

"All fifty of you better be in that school at 1:00 p.m.," I told them. If they didn't know who I was then, they knew after they asked the right people—either they went to school, or they were subject to being stabbed later on. From there I walked back to the school and told them they had people coming at 1:00 p.m., and if they didn't teach them, they were going to have to deal with me. At 1:00 p.m., that classroom was filled. The principal and teacher signed them up, and they took the class while I sat in the corner, continuing to do my work.

One day not too long after that, the teacher told me that an inmate, Craig, was missing. I questioned how he could be missing from prison when the teacher clarified that he hadn't come to class. I walked right back out of the classroom and headed for the yard where I saw Craig walking with two of his buddies.

"What the fuck are you doing?" I asked him. "Get in school. You're on my name. These motherfuckers can't help you." His boys looked at him in a way that told him he'd better move his ass. We walked back through the gates and back to the classroom. After that, I realized that they all needed to see my face. I had to walk down the halls and past the classrooms—stop in and ask the teachers how my guys were doing. Every so often I would go to New Man and ask again about who didn't have a GED and get them to the school. It got to a point where there were so many people going to school that they brought their friends. It was the place to be.

It turned into my first ever "program," and it all grew out of my new attitude. It was nothing I had ever planned for—it sort of just walked into my space. I just had to keep moving forward and trust that I was doing the right thing, and positivity made its way toward me.

It took my being honest with myself to accomplish this. I had to admit that though I was helping these men, I was in some measure doing it to help myself. Putting them in a space to improve themselves made me feel good about myself, and it helped me build a new reputation within the walls of the prison. As I long as I told myself the truth about my motivations—all of them—and forgave myself for it, then good was accomplished for all involved. I couldn't get wrapped up in the idea that I couldn't admit that my motivations weren't completely altruistic, or I never would have done it. My path was too important to sacrifice doing good because I might feel guilty about the reasons I was doing it.

In order to continue my growth, I had to execute on my plan, because there were others that were going to try to keep me the same old Andre. That's where Bob comes in.

CHAPTER SEVEN

EXECUTION AND GROWTH

THE STORY OF BOB

Natan became my guy. Still is today.

I'm on the unit one day and I see a bunch of young gang members bullying some white guy. He's tall—maybe six-foot-six—and older and slow. These kids are really giving him the business, and I hate bullies, for a number of now obvious reasons. I stepped in.

"Leave the guy alone," I told them.

"Why, OG?" they asked.

"I said leave him alone."

They fall back, and the guy—Bob—thanks me. "Dre, I appreciate that. They always give me a hard time." I told him not to worry about it. They wouldn't be bothering him anymore. We went our separate ways. The next day I'm on the unit, we exchange hellos. Then, about a week later, I get moved out of that unit, so I only see him twice a week, at best. Still, we always manage to say hello.

My travels in the prison one day took me to one of the program buildings. I walked by an open door and I saw Bob sitting in the room talking to another gentleman. At first, I walked by, but then turned back to say "hey" to my friend, Bob. I asked him what he was doing.

"We're studying," he said, pointing to his friend. The man with him had a different vibe—almost like an aura about him that I didn't understand.

"What are you all studying?" I asked him.

"Life," Natan said.

"Can I study with you?" He said yes and I joined them at the table. I hadn't fully taken in his friend's appearance—not at first. Then I saw them. The curls in his hair. The black suit. His hat sitting on a chair. The man was an Orthodox Jewish Rabbi. Bob was Jewish. He'd never mentioned it before—not that he needed to. We sat and studied together.

The Rabbi was one of the coolest dudes I'd ever met. We didn't have Rabbis in the hood. Brothers in Boston didn't deal with Jewish people. That is to say I knew nothing about this man or what to expect. Right then, he was just a cool white guy who was teaching me unbelievable lessons while I'm in a space of listening and learning.

I tested him, too. I gave him the business about Germans and the Holocaust. I gave him the business about New York and the perceptions of Jews and money. No matter how much I pushed him, everything that came out of that man's mouth was said with pure love. I could read through bullshit one thousand miles away—I couldn't be conned because I lived and breathed the con. This man had no con in him—just that pure love.

Over the next eighteen months, I saw with him every Wednesday. He came in on his days off just to see me. He taught me respect, accountability, forgiveness, and servanthood—in fact, he taught me how to be human. I'd put myself in the right direction. I had my plan. I'd been on this path for nearly five years when I met him. He was the missing puzzle piece that made the larger picture make sense. He made me understand myself, and how I was doing the right things for the right reasons.

He helped me to better understand what it was I meant to

do. I was good at helping people. I saved Bob. I helped the kids in New Man get started in school. I was doing things for what I thought were all the right reasons, but Natan helped me get my thinking and my heart in alignment— helped me be sure my purpose was clear.

While this was happening, even after five years of staying on the path, there were people still trying to get me to be the old Dre. They gave me a hard time about hanging out with a Rabbi. One inmate in particular pressed me about why I was doing so many programs. They thought I had a hustle going—that there was no way I could be in it for self-improvement. I told him that I had stresses, especially around the relationship with my father.

"You're the smartest guy in prison," he said. "You don't have problems. You're 'that guy.' You do what you want, think what you want, and say what you want. How can you say you have problems? That makes no sense."

I told him about how I went to counseling every morning, and I was going to talk about one of two things. Either I was going to talk about how I didn't get along with my dad and how the drama of it was giving me grief—or I'm going to talk about how I'm now going to be doing a life sentence for stabbing him in the face. Either way, I'm going to counseling. It's going to be up to you what I talk about.

"Yeah, that's fucked up that your father abandoned you, man," he said. "You need to go get that fixed."

My life had become about that: not losing the all-out Andre. Changing, being helpful, and doing the right things didn't mean I had to be weak. It didn't mean I had to let people shit on me and kick me in the face. I would still die for mine—the only difference is now I'm dying for the goal. I'm not going to do it for dope and status. I would die to reach the new goals I had set for myself. If I had to hurt someone to get there? That would have happened, too.

I joined the church about six months before I went home from prison. Gordon Haas, my friend that took me to AA and NA, also took me to a program, Cursillo, for the Catholics. I went through it and got saved. It was the best three days of my life. I started attending church—first a Protestant one, because that's where all the black people were, but I couldn't keep up. They jumped all around. Revelations this. Genesis that. It was too much for me. I went back to Catholic services.

Brothers who wouldn't even come near me before now had the opportunity to talk to me because I'm in the church. One of them came up to me and asked what was up with me and the Rabbi. I told them Natan was my dude. They told me I couldn't roll with Natan because as a

Rabbi, he wouldn't profess that Jesus was Lord, and praise was due to the Lord and Savior. He won't acknowledge that He is risen—that he is sitting at the right hand of the Father. He's going to hell and I shouldn't study with him.

I tried to explain to him why I did, but he started to quote the Bible to me—telling me how he's a Bible scholar and I'm new to all this. I fell back on what is central to me: to protect myself.

"A year ago, you wouldn't come within one hundred feet of me because you were scared. That man that you're talking about took me and he sat with me. He helped me get a better understanding of my life to get me to this point. To the point where I'd even talk to your bitch ass. Wherever he's going in the next life, I would gladly go with him. Now for you? Since you love Jesus so much? We can get you to see him today if that's what you want. Don't you tell me who my friends are because you ain't my friend."

It was important that while I was trying to forge this new life for myself, that I didn't let go of some of the qualities that made me *me*. Ebenezer Scrooge was known to be one thing, but he changed. The Grinch was known to be one thing, but he changed. They both grew. I had to step out of the world I once knew, but I had to take the mindset of being a king and make it line up with the new world I was trying to inhabit. Otherwise, I'd just be a Polaroid—a picture of the person I was trying to be, instead of actually growing to become that person.

CHAPTER EIGHT

SUCCESS (SOLUTIONS BY NECESSITY)

I mentioned before that even though I was the boss at the time of my epiphany, I decided to give that up to the number two guy.

The problem was the number two guy, Trevor, wasn't all that bright.

He did everything ass-backwards and upside down, but I didn't see that as my problem—until it was. Word came where he got into a situation in the visitor's room where he got disrespected. He sends a message back to his main guy on the block that he wants us to take the team and go take care of the guy that disrespected him in front of his wife.

I told his number one guy, a man named Chris, that it doesn't take eight people to take care of one guy. "You go see him and you handle it," I said to him. Chris goes to the man's cell and instead of throwing the first punch, he talks to the guy. He comes back to us now giving us the other guy's side of the story. Since Trevor's man didn't do the job, Trevor didn't want to fight with the guy, either. This would have been fine except an expectation had been set—that this guy wasn't going to get away with embarrassing Trevor. When nothing went down, it sent the wrong kind of message about Trevor and his people.

Trevor had a real compulsion when it came to being the boss. He wanted everyone to "kiss the ring." He had this image in his mind about what it meant to be the king, fueled by too many movies and songs about it. He thought everyone needed to bow down and pay their respects. What he didn't realize was that being the boss meant kissing the babies. He had to be there for his people—to walk them through the hell that they were all in together.

Instead, he was always feuding with the white gangsters. On one occasion I went to the barbershop and Trevor was there, along with the top three white gangsters—two Italians and an Irish guy. The three of them always moved together. This day, when one of them got up out of the barber's chair, Trevor took his seat, jumping the line in front of the other two gangsters. He knew how things worked. He knew the order, but he did it to bully and antagonize them. After some arguing, the white guys get up and leave. Immediately, the hall sergeant came in and begged Trevor to get out of the chair, but Trevor refused. The sergeant and I both knew what was coming. Those gangsters were going back to get their team and they were going to bring them back to the shop.

Trevor was trying to bring me back in.

Without hesitation, I grabbed all of the scissors off the counter. There were two young guys in the shop as well, and I yelled at them to do the same. I moved them into the far corner of the shop.

"Don't you move until I tell you to," I said to them. "When I do, you stab whatever comes through that door." I knew that any minute, those doors would open and in would pour their soldiers, all armed with knives. These young boys were nervous as hell. They were new to the prison, had no idea what was going on, and I was gearing them up for what might end up being the fight of their life.

But those men never came. Trevor sat in that chair and the barber finished his haircut. Now Trevor had to leave.

By himself.

It dawned on him that he now had to return to the cell-block where not only those gangsters were, but all their boys were, too. He looked to me for help, then I thought to myself, "I'm not helping you. I don't even like you." He looked to me again for help and I looked away.

The next day, I sat in the cafeteria at my table away from all the other gangs. After I finished my lunch, I stood to return to the unit. A white inmate we called Tucker walked up on me.

"Dre," he said, "you should head over to the school and get your books, because I heard they just came in." It struck me odd, but I agreed. He walked me to the gate and shouted to the CO on the other side to let me through so I could get my schoolbooks.

While I was getting my books, a riot broke out on the unit. They attacked Trevor.

Tucker knew it was coming. He knew the path I was on and he looked out for me. If I had been on the block, friends with Trevor or not, that was white on black fight. It didn't matter who I was or who I stood with. Only the color of my skin mattered. Tucker wasn't a part of the white gang behind the attack, but somehow, he knew it was coming. For whatever reason, he made the decision to step up and help me any way he could.

He couldn't come right out and say there was going to be a riot.

What stuck out to me even more was that the school was closed at lunchtime—yet somehow, he got them to open the door for me to give me two minutes to go to the school. Those two minutes saved me from being in that riot—and kept me on my path. One of my top soldiers, Skin Tight, got stuck in that riot. To this day, he is still in maximum-security segregation lockdown as a result. That riot happened in 1994.

"COME TALK TO THESE KIDS"

They locked the prison down for about a week. Almost as soon as we came off lockdown, there was another riot, this time between the blacks and the Hispanics. That resulted in another lockdown. Soon after that, three inmates kidnapped a CO and held him hostage. Another lockdown, except we didn't come off it so quickly this time. After four riots back-to-back, they realized they needed to change their system. They started shipping inmates out to different prisons, whether they were involved in the riot or not. If you had a name and a reputation, chances were they were coming for you. They came for me and shipped me off.

At the new prison, I continued to mind my business. I'm

still the low-key boss, but I'm still on my path. I'm taking my classes and continuing to help out other inmates. Out of nowhere, one of the prison administrators came to me and said, "Dre, I need you to come out here and talk to these kids."

Apparently, they had brought some kids in for one of these "scared straight" kind of programs. I went out and gave my talk. The room went dead silent—so quiet that I thought I had done a bad job. What happened was that all of these kids had been fed lies about what it meant to be a gangster. I came out and told it to them from the C-level boss' perspective. The "wannabe" gangsters on the outside were giving them the mail-room version. I gave them a shock to the system.

I liked doing it, but I messed up. I threatened a CO who had taken it upon himself to harass me, and I got myself shipped out to yet another prison.

The next prison was MCI-Norfolk, where Malcolm X—who was my third cousin by marriage—had served his time. When I got there, I was like a child in a kid's museum. I wanted to know which cell was his. I got excited because I knew his life story so well. Maybe something about that gave me further inspiration to stay on track, because I got even more involved in the programs there.

One was called Second Thoughts. They brought in six kids from juvenile detention centers and six inmates and put us in a room together with one outside volunteer. We'd have structured conversations. We'd talk about families and gangs; we'd talk about lockup and the things you'd miss, like the holidays. We had to get them to realize that they were in the same place we were, and if they stayed moving in that direction, they'd be in our seats talking to the next set of juvies.

I worked in this program for the three years I was in Norfolk. Every Tuesday and Wednesday, I'd go to training where they taught me how to talk to kids—how to ask them the right questions to get them to open up. I was already good at communicating with them because I was direct, and it worked—the training helped to refine those skills.

At the end of those three years, I made my parole. As a result, I had to tell the kids that I was going home. They were happy for me, but they wanted to know if I would come visit them. They said their program was right in the hood, so it would be easy for me to do. Then they told me that everyone like me always promised them they'd visit when they got out and they never did. I never forgot what that felt like when I was a child—to be told someone would be there only to have the opposite happen. I promised them I would see them.

A BUMP IN THE ROAD

When I first received my parole, the Department of Corrections refused to acknowledge it. The parole board is a separate entity from the DOC. The board decides who is to be released from prison and the DOC is just a holding entity. The DOC took it personally and decided, "We're not letting this one out." The parole board told the DOC to send me to a minimum-security prison and then release me in three months. The DOC said they would never send me to minimum-security—that I was too dangerous, one of the worst they'd ever seen.

My next step was to go to the classification board, and the deputy there denied me as well. I went to him directly and asked what I had to do to be moved to minimum-security since I had earned my parole.

"You have to wait for me to retire," he told me. "And when I retire, I'm going to leave a note on my desk for the next guy telling him to never let your ass out of here. You'll *never* go to minimum-security."

I was shocked to hear this from him. No more than two weeks before that meeting, he had done a huge favor for me. There was an inmate being released on a Monday after serving twelve years, but his son's birthday was the Saturday before. I went to the deputy and asked if there was any way we could secure an early release for him to see his son. Without hesitation, the deputy wrote it up and the inmate was home by Thursday.

When it came to me going to minimum, he said, "never."

"We have a working relationship in here," he told me. "But that's as far as it goes. I know you. You might have fooled somebody or tricked someone on the board, but not me. I will never send you to minimum-security. Never."

For the next six months, I fought back and forth with the DOC and the parole board. The DOC told the parole board unequivocally that they would lose every piece of paper that they sent them in regard to letting me out. It was that simple to them. They felt I was a menace to society, far beyond anything the parole board had the capacity to understand. They needed to protect civilians from someone like me.

I sat up in my cell one day and said, "God, I hate this place, but if it's your will that I serve here, if that's what you want, then I'll serve here." God let me sit there for another five months. The powers that be tried to get me involved in fights. They put me in cells with people they thought were my enemies. They put me on a block with a racist CO. They kept giving me opportunities to fuck myself. They knew if I ended up in a fight, it would violate my parole. I wouldn't do it.

NOVEMBER 15

They couldn't break me. After seven months, my day came. All the paperwork had been signed. There was nothing more they could do to get around it anymore. I was going to be released.

I got up that morning, the same way I always did. I came out of my cell for morning movements at 8:30. Everyone is in the yard when they begin calling names over the loudspeaker for inmates being released. When my name would be called, my team would come to take me to the gate, then watch me walk through the lobby and to the doors where I would make my way to the outside world. I was to be called as one of the first in the morning.

WE ARE ONE

The way it works in prison, there is a moment when all people who see each other as enemies are one—every morning, during the first count, when they start calling names over the loudspeaker to go home. When they call the names and tell them to report to the front gate, everyone knows you're getting out.

And for that one moment, the entire yard—white, black, Spanish, Crips, Bloods, Aryans—for those five seconds, everyone is on the same page. That is the one time of the day when the entire prison is united because the goal in prison—for everyone—is to get out. Even if the name called is one of your worst enemies, you celebrate, because in that moment, we all win.

I didn't hear my name.

I asked what was going on and they said it had been changed, and that I wouldn't be called until the second count. They were going to make me wait as long as they possibly could. I took it in stride.

Lunchtime came, and they told me now they're going to let me go home *after* lunch—just to fuck me over one last time. We came out of our cells at lunchtime. In Norfolk, every unit eats lunch on the unit—we didn't go to a central cafeteria. There were three hallways that fed into a stair-case that leads to the first-floor chow hall. So, at lunch, everyone is either in the hallway or their cells. When the headcount is cleared, they started lunch.

They cleared the count and the CO yells out, "Norman, bag and baggage!"

I walked down the stairs and into the courtyard. It's empty because everyone is still inside eating. It's just me. As I walked, I looked up to the windows. I saw all the men who came up with me for the last fourteen years. White, black, Hispanic, all looking out the windows at me in the court-yard. I see faces that I know I'll never see again because some of them are doing life sentences. They were the only friends I'd ever known.

Them clapping and cheering for me as I walked towards the gates is something I will never forget. It moved me to silent tears.

The gates opened and I stepped outside. I was terrified. I had just left behind the only people I'd ever called friends, and I was now in a world that hadn't existed to me for more than a decade.

When I first went to prison, my father told me, "There are two ways to do time. You can be in the visitors' room, on the phone, trying to get shout-outs on the radio from the DJ, writing letters and trying to be with your girl—and it will drive you crazy. Or you can focus on you, and you only."

I have always been a super literal person, so when he told me that, that's exactly what I did. I spent fourteen years without visits and almost never talking on the phone. The only thing I could control was me inside those walls. I lived in my own personal snow globe, and there was nothing outside of it. What's incredible to consider is that the distance between the gate and the outside to the lobby was no more than thirty to forty feet. That was as far as I had to travel to be in the free world. The walls of the prison might have been miles long and many feet thick as far as I was concerned—yet a short walk put me on the other side of that wall.

Outside, two men from the program waited for me. We got in their car and they drove me to the parole office. Immediately, the woman sitting behind the front desk there began reading the riot act—she's been doing this job for one hundred years, and this is how things work, etc., etc. I only had one question for her:

"When do I get off parole?" I asked her.

"Three years," she told me.

My paperwork said eighteen months, and I told her so. Her paperwork said three years, and she told *me* so. We argued back and forth about it until she told me she was in charge and could send me back that day if need be. It was at that moment that some of the anger management I had done in the programs inside kicked in. It dawned on me that I had eighteen months to fix this problem. It wasn't something I had to solve now. I told her she was right. She handed me her card and I left, flipping her card in the trash on the way out the door.

CULTURE SHOCK

I went back to the car where the two men were waiting for me. They asked me where I wanted to go. Did I want to see my girl? Did I want to go to McDonald's?

"Take me to the youth center," I told them.

A lot changed in the world in fourteen years. Everything moved so much faster. The automatic teller machines talked to you. The buses and cars talk to you. There were white people in the hood. I couldn't wrap my brain around all this change. I quickly felt overwhelmed and stressed out. I needed to be somewhere I felt comfortable.

They drove me to the youth center—the one I promised to visit when the kids came to see me inside. The minute they saw me, they were hyped up. "Yo, OG!" they shouted. "You came!" The staff used to come to the prison, and they recognized me, as well. Where I had been used to speaking with six children in the prison, they brought out all thirty-five kids from the unit. They sat them in a room with me and I gave them my speech— my life story up to that point. We were there together for more than two hours. When it was over, I went to the program house, got my things settled, and went out to see my family.

The juvenile center wasn't open to visitors at night, and my stress wasn't only around in the daytime hours. I got access to a car, and on those nights when I was feeling overwhelmed with the real world, I'd take the forty-minute drive from the hood to Walpole maximum-security prison. The prison sat such that you could see it from the highway. I would pull off to the side of the road and stare at it.

It would be as late as midnight, and I'd just sit and look. I might have done it four or five times after I was released. I saw the housing units and the lawn. I saw the laundry area where I used to work. Locked doors were my friends. That was my home.

The next day, I asked them to take me back to the youth center to talk to them again. It was the only place I felt safe—a locked facility. The four to six hours I spent there became my decompression time. I was in a place where no one could bother me or confound me with new technology. I ended up going there almost every day, talking to the same group each time. It was just a matter of luck, I suppose, that they never seemed to get tired of what I had to say.

After a few weeks, I started to get comfortable. I didn't feel the need to sit and watch the prison anymore, and I didn't have to go see the kids in the detention center to feel safe, though I still went to talk to them. Unbeknownst to me, as I did this, I expanded and improved upon my ability to speak in public. I couldn't tell those kids the same speech every day.

I became a storyteller by force.

AN ACCIDENTAL CAREER

I didn't know public speaking was a job. I did it for the kids because I promised them I would, and it was great that they seemed to respond to it.

When the kids there got out of lockup, they had to go to a transitional facility—a day treatment center, where they report in. I started going to that reporting center to give talks as well, and that's where I met a man named Tim Allen, a pastor and youth parole officer. We got to talking about a number of things, including the Bible. Eventually he suggested to me a Wednesday community meeting that was hosted by Reverend Smith, better known as Rev.

I showed up to the meeting. I knew no one, so I sat at the corner of a table and listened. There were a number of experts from the city talking about what to do about youth violence and gangs. It was intended to be a one-hour meeting, but at about forty minutes I raised my hand.

Then I proceeded to shred everything they had said because all of it was bullshit.

The room was filled with grown men lying to get money— literally making things up to get funding for their community projects. Of course, people don't take too well to having their money messed with, so they pushed back on what I had to say immediately. There was no arguing with my direct experience. They didn't stand a chance.

I returned the following week, and this time, they were ready for me—or so they thought. They came in with statistics and figures and charts, only to have me debunk everything they had to say. I came back the third week, and this time they'd armed themselves with some of the pastors from the community. I took their arguments apart, chapter and verse. I saw it as a huge waste of time. I never went back.

At least, not on purpose.

As part of my parole, I was part of a program that was supposed to do gang outreach. Sadly, the man who ran the program was also a fake—doing it only to get money. He was a Harvard graduate who had given up his potential career to "come and help the poor kids."

When I came to meet him through the program, he had no idea who I was. My first day there, I saw he had a chart hanging on his wall that listed all of the gangs in the area, complete with names of the members. The head of the program had what he called a seven-year plan to reach all of the gang members. I told him that half of them would be dead or in jail by the time those seven years were up.

He ignored that and went on to explain to me who all of the people on his chart were.

"I know," I told him. "I know all of them."

Within the first three weeks of my living in the program house, every last person on his wall walked through the front door. They all came to pay their respects to me. They came from across the state. When the program manager saw all the people on his list walking in his door, he realized his seven-year plan could be done in less than a month. It should have made him happy—had he been in it for the right reasons.

Instead, it made him angry. He was upset that I disrupted his plan, and we fell out—so much so that he went to my probation officer and complained that I didn't have a job. Because of the level of my crimes, I was on federal probation and state parole. Immediately the probation officer calls me and tells me I need a job. I had signed up at Roxbury Community College as soon as I had been released, so I told the officer I was in school. That wasn't good enough—I had to have a job.

I first found one as a clothes buyer for a company in New York. The director of the program didn't approve—he felt New York was too dangerous for me, that "they weren't Christians" in New York and that it was too unsavory.

Then I found work as a concert promoter. I would be paid to go on the road to provide security and logistics. The director said "no" again—they didn't want me around the devil's music. It wasn't good for my soul.

Finally, a friend of my father was able to help. He provided insurance for cities and state governments. My job was to sign them up. He offered to start me off at $60,000 a year and provide me with my own office. He told me I was smart, and he knew I could do the job well. He was confident that by the end of the year, I'd make double that, with my own team working for me. I was ecstatic. I went back to the program director and told him about the job.

He still told me "no."

"Why?" I asked.

He told me it was because that was too much money for me to make. I couldn't go to New York because it was too dangerous. I couldn't be a concert promoter because I would end up in hell. Now I couldn't sell insurance because I'd make too much money. I found a legitimate job that would pay me more than him—and that drove that director crazy.

He made about forty thousand per year. Here I was, three

months out of prison, with the potential to make triple his salary. In his mind, a job for me was making ten dollars per hour at the local grocery store. I had bucked his plan. He reminded me that God says that we have to be faithful a little bit before we can be in charge of a lot, and that I hadn't been faithful long enough—that I'd waste my money, buying things I shouldn't. I didn't care what he said. I was taking that job.

The director called the head pastor from the church— brought in the big guns. He came in and sat down with us. The director read him his script about all the reasons why I shouldn't take this job—why I *couldn't* take this job. They went on and on, never knowing that I had become a jailhouse lawyer. Once they finished, I spoke.

"So, what you're telling me," I said, "is that based on scripture, I have to be faithful a little before I can be in charge of a lot? If that's the case, then I've got one question: what if $120,000 per year is a little for me? Have you talked to God to ask him what amount of money constitutes 'a little' amount of money to Andre?"

Their silence at that was extremely gratifying—but the gratification was temporary.

They still managed to shut the job down. The director would not let go of the fact that I would be making more money than him and he wouldn't have it—despite the fact that he chose that job, chose that path for himself. At the end of the day, I was at their mercy, and I still had to find a job. One of the pastors felt for my situation and offered me a job as his driver.

As fate would have it, the first meeting I drove him to was at the same location as those Wednesday morning community meetings. This was an evening meeting, however, so I didn't expect to see any of the same people. We walked in together and the pastor who my employer is supposed to meet with saw me and pushed him out of the way. It was Rev.

"Where have you been?" Rev said. "We've been looking for you! Come with me, we need to talk."

The pastor I drove for was confused. "He's my driver," he told Rev. "I'm here to meet with you."

"No, no, no, *this* is the man I want to meet with."

"But we have a 7 o'clock meeting!" he said.

"Push it back!" Rev said, and he hurried me up the steps to his office. "I want you to work for me," he said. "What do you need for me to make that happen?"

Rev still did gang outreach, but he recognized that most of the other pastors were doing their work at a very superficial level. They were going out talking to kids at seven and eight years old, not dangerous grown men with guns. They were talking to kids who were related to the gangsters, not reaching them directly. This pastor knew this and wanted to do more.

"I need money," I told him. "I need cars. And I need to be able to hire the people I want to hire."

"You give me respect in the streets and I'll show you the money," he told me.

"That's easy," I told him.

We held a meeting at the community building—fifteen of us seated at a table. There was shooting the night before and the gangs from Dorchester were going at it. At the meeting was a nonprofit from the west side, claiming that one gang was fighting another, and that they were working with Marcus, the head of one of them. The other nonprofit group claimed that they were working with Tank, the man from the other gang that got shot, and they needed to work together to calm everything down.

Around this time, two men walked into the meeting. I stopped the back and forth and asked one of them to clarify who it was that worked with Tank and his gang. One raised his hand. I turned to one of the men who came into the room.

"Yo, Tank," I asked him. "You know this dude?"

"I've never seen that dude before in my life," Tank said. Apparently, Tank hadn't been shot, because he was sitting right next to me.

I leaned forward. "Now, exactly who do you work with? Because you don't work with him."

The other man that came into the room? That was Marcus. He'd never met anyone in that room before, either.

We had three or four more meetings like that. People would make up stories and names about who they worked with. I'd bring in the actual people and prove them wrong. It wasn't just to make a point. It was to show them that they were doing this wrong—that they needed someone who knew the streets inside and out if they had any hopes of making a difference.

From then on, we'd sit in a meeting and if someone made a mention about a gang and what section they were in, I was on the phone, telling someone from that gang to get themselves over to the community center. They'd walk through that door and sit down. There was no more front-ing. No more lying in the room when Andre was around, because I would expose them—hard. They got by just talking about the work without doing the work. Not any-more. I was bringing the work into the room.

During my first year working there, we became the talk of the city. All the top gangsters were coming to our program, and I started hiring them. Word got out they were part of a team with me—particularly to the OG's.

They came to our center to see a bunch of college kids, well-meaning church folks, and me. I was articulate. I understood measurables. I understood systems. I'm the guy, and I've got the guys who can make the difference at the street level on my team.

I'd ask a funder which area they wanted to work with. They'd tell me they were looking at working with Hillboys. I'd pick up the phone and call the head of the Hillboys. He'd come over and I'd introduce them and let the funder know that if the head of the gang didn't like their plans, it wasn't going to happen.

I created bridges that wiped out the fake middlemen and got things done. It made my boss famous—and rich.

The program raised more than $25 million and achieved

global fame. There hadn't been an outreach like ours in thirty years. It was like we lived *The Godfather Part III*— we actually merged street gangsters with the church. Over the next four years, we worked with the White House, we were in front of Congress, helping to shape international policies. We were no longer only doing speeches at the local level.

All the while, my boss was becoming my mentor, and he was a go-getter. He found his way in every door—not always on the up-and-up—and he was taking me with him wherever he went. He recognized my skill set. He'd take me into meetings where I would just sit and observe. When it was over, he'd ask me for my psychological assessment as to how to break them—a skill I had honed when I was in prison. I didn't see how dangerous it was.

Professor Henry Louis Gates was good friends with Rev— they'd come up together in Harvard. Professor Gates had created an after-school program based on work he had done on the creation of a Black encyclopedia. The program had initially done quite well, but attendance had dropped off. He contacted Rev to see if I could help. He brought us to a large house in Harvard Square where we had dinner with eight other people.

Professor Gates explained the situation with the program and how the kids just stopped coming. I asked him what the kids said about why. He said they brought in a professor from California to figure it out and he couldn't. I asked if that professor talked to the kids. Then he said they brought in two other professors from Chicago and New York. I told them that was great, but did those professors talk to the kids? The kids knew why they stopped coming—did you ever think to ask them?

The kids were being seen like mice in an experiment. You don't ask a mouse what it's like to be shocked. You just observe and record their behavior because you can't get their feedback. Kids aren't mice. You can't just bring in experts to make assumptions about what motivates their behavior strictly based on their actions. You have to interact with them. Ask them questions. Find out what makes them tick.

It was as if I'd turned on all the lights in the room and set off bells. They ushered us out quickly after the dinner was over. I didn't understand what was happening, but the minute we were outside, Rev turned to me and asked me for $200,000.

"What?" I said. "I don't have $200,000."

"I need it," he said. "Give it to me."

"You know I don't have it." I said.

"Oh, really?" he said. "Because that's what you just gave them in there. You gave them $200,000 worth of information. They flew people in from around the world trying to solve the problem you likely just solved. They paid out at least that much money to find the answer you just gave them for some food you didn't even like."

It was then that I truly understood the value of information, and the impact that it could have.

CHAPTER NINE

IMPACT

We did a lot of good in the four years that I was at the nonprofit. The good also came with some bad.

Things got to a point where Rev couldn't control me any longer. My way of thinking was too different from his. He was an academic and a researcher. I just did things, and more often than not, my ways worked. I was able to problem-solve on the fly and do so effectively. Rev couldn't do that, and therefore, he couldn't understand it. He saw it happening in front of his face, but he couldn't comprehend how I did it. He had a problem with the way people listened to me. In his mind, I didn't look like a tough guy. I had men on my staff that looked a lot rougher than I did. He tried to gain insights on people in advance— tried to be in control and be ahead of the game. Ahead of me.

PBS wanted to interview Rev for a national special, a multipart series. Rev did the first interview with them, but when they returned for the next part, he blew them off. They attempted again, only to have the same result. They flew out their group to film, but Rev couldn't be bothered. On one occasion, a member of the nonprofit told me to take them out and show them what we did since Rev wasn't around. I obliged. I did it again when they showed up looking for him and he was nowhere to be found.

The final time he missed a meeting, PBS told Rev that if he didn't show up, they were going to shift to doing the story on me. Rev told them "Andre is nobody. He's just a thug who got out of jail and now works for me." They told him I wasn't nobody—that I was attending classes at Boston College, that I was speaking at Harvard and MIT. I was running all of the programs and I was known throughout the city as the face of their agency. I was a national story.

When white television producers told my boss that *I* was the national story? To him, I became the Antichrist.

Suddenly, he was motivated to show up for filming. The next one they wanted to shoot was at a county jail. However, in county jail, people rotate every ninety days, so no one knew who Rev was. When he told them the name of the center he represented, they responded with, "Oh, you're with Andre!" I had become the face of the center, at least locally. I'd helped them to raise $2.5 million in funding from Senator Ted Kennedy, which Rev took to run the national program. That was our arrangement—I'd handle things on the local front, he took the national side.

My running the local program meant that people were going to know my name and face. Because they turned over people in the jails every ninety days, if you weren't a consistent presence there, no one was going to remember you. Nobody knew who Rev was, so the guy told him he needed to have Andre there tomorrow. Soon after, I received a call from the executive director of the program telling me I needed to be at the prison the next day.

I got there early the next day and sat on a bench and waited. When Rev arrived, he looked at me as if I set his mother, kids, and house on fire, and while it was burning, I had thrown in his pets, just for fun. The media was everything to him—and now I was in his space.

That was the beginning of the end for me.

In Baltimore in 2003, a woman was on the local news complaining about the drug dealers who were selling in front of her house. She was tired of the police never coming to do something about it. The story ran on the six o'clock news. On the eleven o'clock news that day, the same reporter was back at her house—only it had been set on fire and members of her family were dead.

Martin O'Malley, the mayor at the time, called Rev because we were the nation's best crisis team. I took my team out to Baltimore and spoke with the mayor every day. I was out on the street doing outreach and assessments. We were there for almost a week, making great headway—not trying to catch anyone, but to prevent it from ever happening again. We made a lot of progress. Then Rev called and told me to come home.

I didn't understand—so I pressed him. I told him about all the good things we were doing, all the results we were getting. Over and over he told me I needed to come home.

Finally, he told me that he and the mayor couldn't agree on money, and because they couldn't do that, they couldn't have our services. I told him to forget the money. We were saving lives—but he wasn't having it. He ordered me to come back.

I called the mayor and could hear the disappointment in his voice. That car ride back was one of the longest of my life. We had a chance to save people, but because two dudes couldn't agree on money, people were going to die.

Before long, in 2004, he fired me. At this time, I was married, my then-wife was pregnant, and I'm now an ex-offender with no job and a GED to my name. I was still taking college classes at three different institutions—Boston College, Roxbury Community College, and UMass Boston—but I had no degree. What was I going to do?

I started searching online for possibilities. I enjoyed my time speaking with the kids in the juvenile detention centers and at the other venues on behalf of the organization. Not only did I like it, I was good at it. I told my wife that I was going to become a motivational speaker. She thought I was crazy, but it made perfect sense to me. After doing some more research online, I drafted a pitch letter and started to send it out to different organizations.

My wife and I were driving through Vermont when I got the email that said I was accepted to give a speech at a Juvenile Conference in Virginia for five hundred dollars. My wife had a job as a professor, so I had to go alone. The conference paid for my hotel and travel. I was ecstatic. Around midnight, I was in my room and decided to walk down to the ballroom where I'd give the speech. I wanted to see the space beforehand and get a feel for it. All the chairs were set up. I walked the stairs to the stage and turned around to face the chairs. One thought crossed my mind.

Dad, I made it.

A tear ran down my face. As much as I wanted to disconnect from him—to not know him or be around him, at the end of the day, I was genetically connected to him. He was my father.

That tear was for *us*—not for him.

EVERYONE NEEDS HELP

The next day, I came down to the ballroom. There were a number of other professional speakers there. They wore nice suits with cuff links.

I crushed them all. I wasn't there to talk about research and statistics. I talked about what was real and the audience ate it up, because no one had talked to them in that way before. I didn't hold back—and it was just the beginning. I was asked to speak at a number of different venues about gang violence, youth programs, and juvenile detention reform.

At one of these speeches, a woman came in to evaluate my speech. She told me it was great, but that I was denying some kids of what I had to offer—specifically white kids.

I told her that rich white kids didn't need me. Poor black

kids did. This country belonged to the white kids. They own it. They own all the sports teams. They own all the businesses. They control the White House. This is pre-Obama. They had it all.

She told me that I didn't understand—that I was the best outreach worker in the city, and that even though I didn't want to work with them, those kids needed me, too. Not only did they need me, but the parents needed me—and they wanted to pay me.

She insisted, so I went to speak to one of the wealthiest suburban schools and I was astounded at what I discovered. They did drugs at the white kid school. They drank at the white kid school. They had sex at the white kid school. There were bullies at the white kid school. There were kids that weren't as smart as the other white kids. There were kids who cut their arms. That didn't connect to their parents.

"But you have fathers!" I said to them.

"You mean the guy who sits upstairs all the time?" they'd answer back. "He doesn't know me. He doesn't even interact with me. He's always on his phone. Always worried about his work and his business. Not me."

I walked out of there with an entirely new perspective.

All kids have problems, regardless of the color of their skin. It's hard being fifteen no matter who you are. I told myself that I would help anyone, anywhere. I'll never deny anybody my assistance based on my ignorance again. From that day forward, I did work at any school that would have me.

"I DID GOOD"

On a flight home from Philadelphia, I discovered a new audience that needed my help.

I met a man named David. We got to talking on the plane. We exchanged information and went to lunch from time to time. It was during one of those lunches that he told me that I needed to start speaking to executives at Young Presidents' Organization (YPO) conferences. Though I had promised myself not to be limited by my bias, I slipped into my old habits.

"Why would rich CEO's need me?" I asked. "That doesn't make sense. I need to help kids who are dying, on drugs, and getting shot."

Dave wouldn't hear it. We met for lunches regularly over the course of a year, and he finally convinced me of the need to do it. He believed that my story and message was crucial to this audience, and they would pay me well to hear it—very well. Dave also knew that that kind of money would give me the opportunity to fund whatever it was I wanted to do to help people. He told me that he felt bad about being rich and he was going to give me the platform to change the world, not just because it was necessary, but he was honest enough to tell me it would help him alleviate the guilt he felt at being so wildly successful. I was his "I did good" project—and I was all right with that.

I did my first YPO speech in Boston, and again I crushed it by bringing a reality to a speech that that audience had never heard. From there, I went on to do a speech for the Global Leadership Conference (GLC). What made this speech so terrific for me was that while I was in town for a speech, I would also do one to two days of volunteer work. I was able to go out and give two to three free speeches for the local community before going to the large executive conference. It gave me the opportunity to do outreach in cities other than my own. I would hold events in juvenile detention centers, public schools, county jails, or foster care centers—any place that needed exposure, and where I felt comfortable. I brought CEOs in to meet principals of underserved schools and juvenile court judges—people who would probably never meet otherwise. It was a fantastic opportunity to bring those two worlds together, and to expand my outreach outside of my Boston bubble.

A number of successful speeches with YPO led to an invitation to give one in Sweden. I had been in prison for fourteen years, and now I was going to do a six-day tour. The speech was a wild success, so much that one CEO in particular insisted that I return for a one-month engagement. He organized the entire tour which had me running all over the country. One of the days while I was there, the CEO invited me to lunch in his home.

It was a beautiful home, the nicest house in the nicest part of town. He had every luxury you could imagine—things he didn't need, vehicles he didn't even use. What was remarkable about him, though, was that he never presented himself in that way. In fact, had I not been to his home, I would have never known how wealthy he actually was.

He took me for a walk after lunch. His home was an oceanfront property, and we strolled on frozen water.

"I have to ask you," I said to him. "You can buy anything you want. At this point, you probably have. I've had this idea in my mind as a kid that when I grew up, I would buy a house, a car, a boat, a plane, just buy, buy, buy. But that was just a dream. You've actually done it. You've reached the level where there's nothing you can't buy. What do you do next?"

He didn't think long before he answered. "I want to consolidate all of my businesses and devote my life to actually making a difference in this world. I want to make an impact. Why do you think you're here? It's so I can learn from you."

When he said that, his words hit me like a liver shot.

Everyone wants to be rich, even the people who don't talk about it. So, when you meet one of the richest guys in the country and he tells you that he wants to be like you, it takes the wind out of you. How do you handle that kind of information? All this time, my goal had been to be this CEO—and now his goal was to be like me.

It was then that I realized that I was where I was supposed to be. I didn't need to focus on being rich, because having everything meant nothing if you couldn't make an impact. It caused me to think about people like Oprah, Bill Gates, and Warren Buffett. They've all reached that stage where they've become philanthropists. They also realized that there is an intersection where they reached the top of the hill, and now it's time to make a difference.

My opportunity to make a real impact would come soon after—an opportunity that completed my journey from the prison yard to the Harvard yard.

CHAPTER TEN

CRISIS MANAGEMENT

Dave and Suzie Spence were YPO members that I met through a speech I gave in St. Louis, Missouri. They were very successful with a wonderful family. Suzie had been in St. Louis, volunteering for years. During my outreach week while speaking, I went to give a talk at Roosevelt High School. The kids flipped out with excitement as they had heard about who I was. When Suzie heard I had visited the school and had a great success, she invited me to their home.

There she told me about the organization she works with to help improve the school, called Care. They told me everything that they were doing, and I could see that while they were trying their hardest, their strategies were not going to be all that effective. After they presented,

Suzie asked me to tell them what I thought. I told them what I saw and how I thought they could improve, not knowing that Suzie had been telling them this behind the scenes all this time.

Afterwards, she took me into her kitchen and said, "Andre, you have to come here. You have to work with me and with these kids. You have to come and make our efforts better." She had so much determination in her voice and in her eyes, in a way I hadn't seen in others who did the kind of work she did. We clicked immediately and I had no choice but to say yes. For the next ten months, Dave and Suzie invited me to live in their home. I took their kids to school. I became the cool "uncle." I was part of the family.

In the evenings, I'd go out to bars and restaurants. I'm a person that likes to talk to people, and so I'd strike up conversations wherever I could. In doing so, I'd meet lawyers, sometimes, and tell them about the work we were doing at Roosevelt High. Then I'd call Suzie and tell her I was bringing them back to the house to meet her. She'd set up wine and cheese and entertain them while we talked about the efforts we were making. Other times, I'd meet gang members, and she would entertain them as well. Other times, it was physicians. Anyone we thought could help to further our cause, to volunteer their time at the school, or—at the very least—to raise their awareness of the issues there.

It became so frequent that Dave and Suzie had to take turns hosting because they couldn't keep staying up late as they had to work the next morning. No matter what, they had complete trust in what I was doing. They'd lend me their nicest vehicles to go out to even the worst neighborhoods to recruit people to our project. They were totally committed.

No matter where I went, I had Roosevelt High School on my mind. There were gangs in the school, so I needed to understand how the gangs there operated. If I was out to the movies, out at the mall, what have you, I'm looking to find gang members. I had one sole mission, no matter who I met: I wanted to find a way to connect them in a beneficial way to Roosevelt High School.

The gang members were always impressed when I brought them to Dave and Suzie's home. They couldn't believe I "lived" there, and because they were so impressed, they were happy to sit down and kick it with me. Suzie always had a story and a smile for them, and she made them feel right at home.

In those ten months, we turned that school around. Prior to our work there, there was a significant gang presence in the school and teachers who were checked out. There were fights in the hallway. There was no accountability—for anyone. There were no systems in place. It was, in a sense, all bad.

I walked through the school and looked at everything that would prevent a child from learning, and everything that would make a teacher not want to teach. I walked into the teachers' bathroom and it was absolutely disgusting. It looked like one you'd find at a roadside gas station. One of the first things I did was have those bathrooms remodeled. These teachers were in a school where kids were getting mugged, stabbed, and shot. Cleaning up a filthy bathroom was the last thing on their mind, not to mention the fact that it was demoralizing every time they walked into it.

That was just the start. We built a medical clinic on-site, that included mental health services and dental services. We put tutors in the in-school suspension area, so kids weren't just locked in a room with nothing to do. We secured a federal internship.

When the time came, I made my leave. I met incredible people during those ten months. Along with Dave and Suzie, I was fortunate enough to meet many people and form lasting friendships. It was truly a life-changing experience on a number of levels.

FERGUSON

Our work with Roosevelt High School finished up in 2012.

Two years later, Michael Brown, Jr. was shot in Ferguson.

I don't remember where I was when it happened, but I remember that the world went crazy. The riots and protests were all over television. All the people who knew me from St. Louis began calling me.

That was before the grand jury's non-indictment. When that happened, Ferguson exploded. A St. Louis EO member and friend, Dan Curran, reached out to me and told me they absolutely needed me. People were going to get hurt. I jumped on a plane immediately and had a meeting with Dan to come up with a plan. Dan shot video, so I told him we were going to take his camera down to Ferguson.

We went down there at approximately midnight. I knew some of the people involved in the protests from my work at Roosevelt. They weren't the main guys, but they were able to get me in the loop. The protestor had arranged a Twitter meetup of sorts—they'd send out a tweet to their followers and then they'd organize a spot to get together. I showed up with a white CEO and a video camera—and I started talking to people.

I asked them why there were there and for what purpose. My questions eventually got me to speak with the leadership of the movement, one of the men spearheading it all. In that conversation, I asked him what a win looked like for him out of all of this. He told me a rec center. On camera, I told him:

"You have the world watching you ask for a fucking recreation center? We ask for something global."

I told them that I was going to bring them all to Harvard, and when I do, we'll have a meeting and discussion around making this better—not just about what's wrong. We're going to come up with solutions to fix it. They agreed.

I went back to Dave Spence and told him I needed his help. He reached out to the mayor of Ferguson, as well as the police chief. He flew them to Cambridge. In the meantime, I went to New York to get some of Eric Garner's family, another man who had died at the hands of the police—for selling cigarettes—and brought them to the conversation as well.

We got the protestors, the mayor and the chief of police of Ferguson, and Dave Spence all in the same hotel. They'd been battling for months but we'd got them all under one roof. I got them all to a panel that I organized with people I chose. I was going to moderate it, because I knew things would not get out of control if I did.

Things weren't that simple.

A young woman from Ferguson who was a law student at Harvard had become something of a mini-celebrity. She got wind of the Ferguson panel and became upset when she discovered she had nothing to do with it. She went to the law office and lodged a complaint about the meeting because she wasn't a part of it. She felt that members of the panel, particularly the mayor and police chief, had no right to speak for Ferguson. She ignored the fact that the panel also included people from the neighborhoods—that both voices were represented.

Regardless, the head of the program conceded—to the point where he was going to cancel the panel. Dr. Charles Ogletree, thankfully, stepped in and told him that was ridiculous—that this was national news. So, to find a middle ground, they put the young lady on the panel. She didn't want to be there by herself, so she convinced them to add another activist, and another one of her associates out of D.C.

The panel starts and everyone is grandstanding. All of these extra people that were added on had their own agendas. The people I had chosen had one: solutions. One of the women who had been added gave a fifteen-minute introductory speech that was useless. Then she passed the mic to the activist who again only spoke about the things that benefitted her.

Once that was done, we finally got to the panel discussion. The young woman who protested her way onto the panel made sure she was sitting next to the mayor, likely for the photo opportunity. When she asked someone a question from the side he was representing, she turned her back on him as he answered—her own form of grandstanding. I was disgusted.

It went off the rails from there. The protestors—who I'd prepared to come to talk solutions—had now gone the other way. They're in activist mode, not problem-solving mode. The head of the protestors started yelling, even swearing at the mayor and his people. He did a spoken-word piece where he slammed them all to their face.

I tried to manage it as best as possible, but it was a slaughter. There was no win for City Hall at this point, because they were getting shit thrown at them from all angles. The crowd was already against them—now the panel was against them, too. I was deeply embarrassed, because I didn't bring them there for that. They knew it wasn't my fault, but at that point, it didn't really matter. They were furious.

When it was over, Dr. Charles Ogletree—Barack Obama's mentor and the head of the Charles Hamilton Houston Institute at Harvard Law School—invited the original members of the panel to all have dinner together.

We all sat together at the restaurant, but there were

enough of us that we took up two tables. The lead pro-testor had taken a spot at the second table, so I pulled up next to him and asked him what had happened. Did he want justice for his people? Did he want things to get better? It wasn't going to happen like that.

"If you want to solve the problem," I told him, "you're going to have to *talk* to them. They control the city, and the way you spoke to them, you would have thought they were a dog in the street. If anyone of them had talked to you that way, there would have been a fight. The mayor, the police chief, they can't hit you because of their posi-tion. You don't have to like him, but you *do* have to talk to him like a man. You can't speak to him the way you did and expect a conversation. You need to walk over there, not to apologize for what you said, but the way you said it. Then start a dialogue that's going to take you to a solution. Agree to disagree on some things, then find the places you *do* agree and work it out the rest of the way."

He stood up and walked over to the mayor, the police chief, and Dave. He said, "I want to apologize for the way I said what I said. I meant all of it, but the way I spoke to you was wrong. You're grown men and I need to speak to you as such." They shook his hand, he sat down, and they began talking—right there over dinner. Soon, the other protestors joined in and they're all having conversations about how to fix the situation in Ferguson.

When they flew home and returned to Ferguson, they communicated with each other. They still had organized protests, but the police knew when and where they would be. They didn't show up with rubber bullets and tear gas because the protests were peaceful. They were able to make their voices heard and no one got hurt because they had all come to an understanding over that dinner.

CHARLES OGLETREE

Professor Charles Ogletree is the head of The Hamilton Institute for Race and Justice at Harvard.

He saw the whole meeting going off the rails and how it was going to stay off the rails, and he saw the discouragement and defeat in my face. He pulled me aside and said:

"Andre, get everybody together—not the other ones, only the people you brought—and I'm going to take you all out to dinner. This is a chance to get your plan back on track. It's never over until it's over. Don't give up. Round them all up and we'll get another chance. Don't throw in the towel."

That dinner gave me the chance to mend the fences. Had that second meeting not happened, Ferguson might still be burning down.

The lead protestor, eight months after the panel at Harvard, ran for office and is now a state representative in Missouri. At the time of writing this book, he now sits with the governor to talk about crime policy and how to make Ferguson a safer place to live.

MAKING IT TO HARVARD

As a result of my work setting up the panel and bringing the two sides of Ferguson together, I was granted a Harvard Fellowship. They allowed me to bring the whole thing together under their auspices. Once they issued me my official email, I knew I had made it.

I went from the prison yard to Harvard yard, exactly as I had said I would.

I had been there at the fringes from my work with Rev. I had spent time on campus and even done a speech once when he was unable to make it. Subsequently, I'd done additional speeches at the John F. Kennedy School, the Law School, and the Divinity School. I attended events with Cornel West, Charles Ogletree, and the aforementioned Henry Louis Gates. Even with all of that, I hadn't felt like I'd truly accomplished my goal.

But with the Ferguson program, it was official—I had become a Harvard Fellow. In many ways, it felt even more meaningful than attending as a student, because I had earned my way in doing what others told me they couldn't do—by making an impact. As a result of that work, I was able to meet Michael Brown, Sr. and I mentor him to this day.

Looking back, I see that everything I had been through up

to that point had led to that moment. It would have been easy in the face of the adversity of that train wreck of a panel to give up. I'd been taught, long ago, that giving up was okay. Had I done that, the ramifications could have been a catastrophe. Instead, by staying the course, by fostering communication and conversations, we bridged what seemed like an impossibly huge gap that resulted in a decrease in violence and a hope for real change.

I had achieved my goals. Gone were the days of sitting in a cell with shackles on my hands and feet, committing my life to nothingness—being the king of nowhere.

EPILOGUE

PUTTING DIRT ON THE GRAVE

Getting the fellowship from Harvard was, in theory, the happiest day of my life.

In theory.

It was the culmination of a dream, one that had morphed from attending Harvard to working there. Everyone applauded. I told people on every social media outlet, "Look at me, I made it. I am the ultimate success story. The OG who made good. From the prison yard to the Harvard Yard, and a fellowship at the law school."

I worked with London Business School since 2001. My mentee got a White House appointment along the way. I'd done the impossible, and for the record, I've done it multiple times. I did the Babe Ruth—I called my shot and put it right in the upper deck.

What the world didn't see was that I was in the middle of a divorce. I missed my son. They didn't see the dysfunction in my family. That I was still getting grief from my mother, father, brothers, and sisters. The world didn't see that all of these things were bearing down on me. The truth was that when I was fighting for my goals, I could ignore all of those things. Now that I'd achieved what I'd set out to do, I couldn't ignore it anymore.

If you've won the marathon, what keeps you going to the gym the next day? Achieving the impossible took some of the purpose of my day away. It let my life's ills worm their way back in, because I wasn't running as fast as I was before. I wasn't running at all. All the things I could have and should have done better, they caught up with me.

I was as sad as I was happy—maybe more so. Outwardly, my life looked great. Inside was horrible. Much in the way the world thought Freddie Prinze, Kate Spade, or Anthony Bourdain had it all before they killed themselves, they had no clue about their internal suffering. When they came to a point where they weren't filming the show or playing on stage or going to an opening, they were no longer protected from their demons. When the noise dies down, you're vulnerable and you can't hear the laughter.

My demons came for me, and they came for me hard. I gave up.

I took off and moved out of the country. It was a place where I thought I could run away to where my demons couldn't catch me. What it was, in fact, was a symbol that my life had gotten out of control. If I had been in control, I would have been home holding my wife and son. I would have been in church, doing work in the community. Instead, I moved to the Virgin Islands. I wanted to be by myself.

I lived alone for six years, because I didn't want to see or talk to anyone. At home, every day was about me giving. Don't misunderstand, I love the giving. It's what drives me—but there was no getting. As my marriage fell apart, my wife moved to Africa. My mother and father were still a source of pain and frustration, and my brothers and sisters were as well.

So, I retreated. My plan was to hide in obscurity, maybe for the rest of my life. I'd do some appearances from time to time and then head right back to the islands. Even when I was there, I spent eighty to ninety percent of the time in my house. I spent almost all of my time alone, which was not a good thing for me. Even today, I work twenty hours a day because I can't stand to be home alone. I had always had a hard time connecting to people. So there I was. I was back in prison—just one of my own making.

Though I thought I had a hard time connecting with people, I was wrong. The people I'd met along this journey—Keith, Dave, Suzie, Dan, and a list of others—after four and a half years, they realized that I had tapped out, and they weren't going to let me do that. I spoke to them periodically and they knew from those conversations that something was deeply wrong.

They got together and spent the next eighteen months reaching out to me, never giving up. Phone calls, email, texts—anything they could do to stay involved in my life. I didn't want to come back to reality, though. I stopped doing the speeches, the outreach, and the programs. I walked away from the fellowship and a lucrative corporate speaking career. I walked away from it all, locked into a depression that I couldn't escape.

And then, the persistence of my friends broke through my prison wall. It was no one message, or one photo. It was the fact that I had lived a life where no one cared about me—until now.

I'd been on my own forever. Me taking care of me was all I had ever known. Even when I was having these successful speaking engagements, I was by myself. People loved the stories. People loved the energy. But when it came to me stopping the events, there were a number of people that said, "If he doesn't want to be on stage, we don't need him." Many people faded away. Most people couldn't be bothered. No one cared.

Except they did. Those people I mentioned became true friends—and for eighteen months straight, they wouldn't let me forget it.

As a result, I came out of that funk a changed man. I knew now that there were people in my life who truly, truly cared about me. They didn't just tolerate me. They were with me because they chose to be, not because they had to be. These people are part of the uber-successful elite. Super wealthy. They could be friends with anyone. They chose to say, "Andre is our friend." They didn't do it for what they gained from our relationship. They did it because they were invested in my well-being—because they loved me.

I won't lie—it took me some time to accept it, because I had rejected the concept of people caring about me for so long. It just didn't make sense to me. People not caring about me had been a driving force me throughout my life. I could do anything because I had to—because it was what was good for Andre. I had no one to answer to but myself. I could do good or bad—I could do whatever I wanted. If Andre dies? Who cares?

They did.

Even with all that love, I was still only about halfway out of the hole, because I wasn't doing what I was supposed to do—I wasn't living my purpose. They flew me out to St. Louis to have a meeting. Attending it were Rusty Keeley, Dave Spence, Dan Curran, John O'Leary, John Ruhlin, and Keith Alper. They asked me what I was doing since I'd returned home, and I told them I was selling real estate in Atlanta.

"That's not what you do," they told me. "That's not who you are."

They told me I had to go back to living the life I had created for myself. They formed a board, just for me—the Andre Norman board, designed to get me back to where I was supposed to be. They made it so I checked in with them every month to make sure I was on the path to being successful again—not just in terms of money. They wanted to be sure that I was living my purpose again. They kept their word. They made phone calls. They held meetings. They checked in regularly. They forced me to be accountable to them—in the best way possible.

The result?

Today I work at Genius Network, the number one mastermind group in the world, with my brother, Joe Polish. I'm a Fellow at Harvard Law School under Charles Ogletree, mentor to Michelle and Barack Obama. I'm the founder and director of Academy of Hope, a housing unit for the most violent offenders in the Department of Corrections, and to my knowledge, never before has a former prison gang leader been given such controls. Since that program has been open, we've not had one fight or staff assault. I'm a consultant to governments regarding social impact in cities. I have a contract to create motivational content for hundreds of thousands of prisoners. And I'm the corporate trainer for the London Business School's Executive Education department.

The list quite literally goes on and on.

Through all of this, I discovered the enjoyment in sharing. Before, I'd metaphorically save a kid in a well or pull someone out of a building and then go home alone to a microwaved dinner. Now I have people I can call that I know care about what I'm doing. Where I once saw myself as a burden, I now know and understand that the people that helped get me back on the path genuinely care about what I'm doing. It's a feeling that is hard to describe.

IT'S DONE, AND IT'S DONE RIGHT

There was one man out of the group that went above and beyond more than any other. That man was Keith Alper.

What I didn't know was that while Keith was leading the team, his wife, Nancy, was in the hospital fighting cancer. I had never met her. I only heard the wonderful stories about her. It wasn't until I received the email from Keith that she had passed that I was even aware that she had been sick. Only then did I hear the stories from others that knew Keith and his wife that she'd been in the hospital. That her cancer had gone into remission and then returned. Her last two years overlapped with the time that he'd been working with me, trying to save me.

I would have understood completely if he had said, "Andre, you're a great friend, but this woman is the love of my life. She is the mother of my children. I need to be there for her, twenty-four hours a day, seven days a week, because it's all I've got left with her." He never made that an option. He drove the bus for me because that's who he is.

After I received the email, I flew out for the service. It was incredible. I've never seen so many people at a funeral in my life. It was a testimony to the life she'd lead. Nancy was everyone's favorite aunt; everyone's favorite sister; everyone's favorite camp counselor. Everyone's favorite everything. There must have been 1,000 people in attendance.

We left the service and went to the graveyard. It had been

raining at the time. At the gravesite, they continued the service. Keith and his kids were distraught. The most wonderful woman they'd ever known has died. During the service, the rabbi told us that the greatest mitzvah that you can do for someone is to place dirt on their grave—because they can't pay you back.

The people in attendance began to place dirt on her grave. The rain started pouring in buckets. The dirt mound next to the grave turned to mud. There were elderly people there trying to shovel the heavy mud, but it was too much for them to handle. The rain fell so hard that it was difficult to even hear the rabbi. It was so heavy that the rabbi called an end to the services. We had paid our respects. He sent everyone home—but the grave was only half full.

I sat in my car while everyone drove off. All I could think of was what this woman had done for me, a man she had never met. I got out of my car, walked back up to her grave, and I shoveled the dirt in until the grave was full. I couldn't think of leaving it half done. I had never met Nancy, and I never will, but if she hadn't given Keith permission to save me, it could have just as easily been me in that grave.

I pulled out my phone and texted Keith.

It's done, and it's done right.

The next day there was a shiva service at Keith's house. I went and found a seat apart from the crowd. Everyone in the building knew Nancy but me. Eventually more than one person approached me and asked, "How did you know Nancy?"

"She was my angel," I told each and every one of them.

No one ever questioned it.

A BASKET OF PEBBLES

About three hours into the Sunday service, I could see that Keith was surrounded by family and friends. No one was crying. They were enjoying the fond memories of Nancy, and I could see that he was in as good a spirits as he could be. I walked over and gave him a hug and told him he was in good hands. He insisted that I stay, but I knew it was my time to go.

Nancy died on my son's birthday. When the time came for her gravestone dedication one year later, I explained to my son that I had to make this trip.

When they had her dedication, there was a basket of pebbles where everyone draws a pebble and places it on top of the gravestone. When everyone had said their prayers and was about to leave, I noticed that the basket was still half full of stones. I asked them, "Do you need these anymore?" When they told me "no," I took them with me.

Looking at those stones, I realized that any one of them could have been placed on her grave. These were hers. They couldn't be thrown away. I took them home. To this day, they sit in a special place in my home. They sit in that same basket on my shelf. Every year, when I visit her grave, I bring one of those stones. There are more stones left in that basket than I have years left on this planet, but I will take one there every year until that time comes.

Last summer, I sat my son down and told him the story of the stones. He'll get them when I die, along with the Bible I used the week I got saved, and the Jewish Psalm book I was given by my rabbi's wife. They are the three most special things I own. When I get the chance, I'll fly him out to the gravesite so he can meet the woman who gifted me a second chance to be the best person I could possibly be.

MY MITZVAH FOR YOU

It is my sincere hope that this book can be a mitzvah for those who read it—a favor for which I expect no return. I pray that my story speaks to you in ways that inspire and motivate you to overcome whatever challenges you might be facing. Whether you've faced imprisonment and poverty as I did, or if you're an executive struggling to find meaning in your place in the world and how you can make an impact, take comfort in the fact that you are *not* alone. There is someone out there who has been where you are—in one way or another—who perhaps can be the second voice to pull you out of the depths of whatever pain you might be experiencing.

Now that we are friends—and we are now since you've read my book—I want you to reach out to me at hope@andrenorman.com or www.andrenorman.com.

Tell me *your* story.

Tell me how I can help *you*.

* * *

A LETTER TO
MY FATHER

Dear Dad,

I have been very disappointed with you and our relationship for most of my life now; thinking of the times when I needed you most only to find myself alone without your support or guidance. This book could never describe the hurt or pain that I endured. I was focused on my truth and lessons to help others rather than your feelings.

The morning I approved the manuscript to be sent off for final edits and printing, I was so happy to be finished with this project. It's been a long time coming. My prison program, Academy of Hope, had a guest speaker on that same afternoon. Pastor John Gray shared a message about grace, forgiveness, and his dad. It was one of those "this message was exclusively for me" days.

Shifting from "my truth" to "the truth," the facts are that I also caused hurt, pain, and disappointment, too. Through all of my faults I have been forgiven and given a second chance—yet I had been unwilling to do the same for you. It is much easier to tell others that forgiveness is powerful and necessary than doing it myself.

You're my father and I want to appreciate you for doing the best you could with what you had. I've always only wanted to make you proud and earn your respect. Well, Dad, I have done good. I survived all that the world could throw at me and I am still standing tall, carrying our family name. I am the Ambassador of Hope. It wasn't easy but I made it. I pray that you are truly proud of me, and know that throughout it all, I never wanted another dad. I just wanted more of you.

I will focus on the time we have left rather than the time that has gone by. We have a lot to catch up on. I am looking forward to getting to know the new you and sharing with you the new me.

I love you. I miss you. And I forgive you.

Your Son,

Andre

ACKNOWLEDGMENTS

I would like to offer special thanks to Cameron Herald and John Ruhlin, who are great friends of mine. They knew my story and were adamant about it being told, during the Genius Network annual event they introduced me to Tucker Max and Scribe. Without their love and compassion, this story might never have been written.

Additional thanks go out to the following people, in no particular order:

Mom, Dad, Keith Alper, Natan Schafer, Suzie Spence, David Spence, Benjamin Richter, Rusty Keeley, Dan Curran, John O'Leary, Kenneth D. Merin, GOT Family, Father Martin, Joe Polish, Jeff Ward, Cursillo #293, Michael Maddox, Felix Stubbs, YPO Family, Gordon Haas, David Seligman, Randy Cohen, Dr. Ben Hardy, Maureen Walsh, Jason Fladien, Jules Goddard, Todd Johnson, Andy

Buyting, Sean McAdam, Fernando Castillo, Greg D'Amico, Nanna Palmas, Diana Aubourg, Garnett Littlepage, Mrs. Oliver, Jim and Mimi Dew, Cesar R. D'jesus, Mrs. Ellis, JT McCormick, EO Family, Simon Nynens, Jose Solis, Anthony Norman, Judge David S. Nelson, Deacon John McMillan, Eric Norman, Auntie Tina, Nancy King, Genius Network Family, Kim Comeau, Paolo Garzaroli, Morgan Zalkin, Robert Henderson, Sam Qurashi, Larry Sagen, Michael and Debra Bernoff, James 1840 Skinner, Will Dunn, Judge Paul Chernoff, Mattapan Family, Mr. Bowtie, John Vercher, Bishop Robert Perry, Sister Ruth, Sister Kathleen, Pastor Tim Allen, Imani Husbands, Patrick Dempsey, Naomi Winbush, Mark Thomas, Nanna Norman, Brian Hall, Uncle Kingston, Auntie Kate, Cousin Christopher, Janine Winbush, Dominic Williams, Eva Norman, Per-Olof Soderberg, Father Martin, Michelle Lemmons-Poscente, Brock Coleman, and Brianna Davis.

ABOUT THE AUTHOR

After fourteen years as one of the most feared men in the Massachusetts prison system, ANDRE NORMAN discovered his purpose, appealed his sentence, was granted parole and returned to the world a changed man. As the Ambassador of Hope, Andre's work was instrumental in bringing an end to the protests in Ferguson, Missouri—work that earned him a fellowship at Harvard University. In addition, Andre utilizes his unique understanding of everyone from corporate executives to prison inmates to help them find their purpose and turn their lives around. He is a highly sought-after motivational speaker and serves as a consultant for executive groups, prison systems, and nonprofit organizations.

CPSIA information can be obtained
at www.ICGtesting.com
Printed in the USA
FSHW011653260420
69617FS